THE CHANGING FACES OF
West Oxford

D0528879

Malcolm Graham

Robert Boyd
PUBLICATIONS

Published by
Robert Boyd Publications
260 Colwell Drive
Witney, Oxfordshire OX8 7LW

First published 1998

Copyright © Malcolm Graham and
Robert Boyd Publications

ISBN: 1 899536 24 8

All rights reserved. No part of this book may be produced, stored in a retrieval system, or transmitted, in any form or by any means, electronic, mechanical, photocopying, recording or otherwise, without the prior approval of the publisher.

OTHER TITLES IN THE *CHANGING FACES* SERIES

Printed and bound in Great Britain at The Alden Press, Oxford

Contents

Cover illustrations

Front: Youngsters on the diving boards at Tumbling Bay, 1959.

Back: Coronation fancy dress competitors at Botley Road

Nursery, 1953.

Acknowledgements

I would like to thank the many people who have helped me with this book by sharing their memories and pictures of West Oxford. They include John Alden (JA), Ann Allan (AA), Bob Allen, Malcolm Axtell (MA), Tom Ballance, Ken Barratt, Edith Bartlett, Joan Bates, Greta Betts, Bill Bowell, Pamela Bower, Chris Broadway (CB), Norman Bunning, Brendan Carter (BC), Don Chapman, Ken Charlwood, Donald Cross, Jeremy Daniel (JD), 'Dick' Dodson, Mike and Pat Ferrett (MPF), Frank and Ethel Fowler, Charles Gee, Renie Haffenden (RH), Francis Harris (FH), Gwen Ilsley, John and Richard Jeffery (JRJ), Mike Jenkins (MJ), Leslie Jones, Thomas Henry Kingerlee, Jenny Lindsell (JL), Pauline Milward (PM), Bill Munsey (BM), Vernon Orr (VO), John Power, Gillian Sawyer (GS), Pat Stansfield (PS), Bill Stevens, Mel Summers, Jim Tyler, David Walker (DW), Mary Walton (MW), David and June Warne (JDW), Laurence Waters (LW), Jill Wilson and Maurice Woodward (MWO). Adelaide Barrington, formerly Librarian at the Oxford and County Newspapers Library (OCN), and her staff were very helpful in giving me access to photographs and newscuttings. The initials after some names indicate those who have kindly loaned their photographs and allowed me to use them; these initials appear at the end of each relevant caption.

I am most grateful to Keith Price, Picture Editor at Oxford and County Newspapers, for permission to reproduce photographs from the firm's library and to Mary Clapinson, Keeper of Western Manuscripts at the Bodleian Library, University of Oxford (Bodl.) for permission to reproduce three images. I would also like to thank the Imperial War Museum for permission to reproduce one photograph from its collection.

All the other photographs are from Oxfordshire County Council's Photographic Archive and copies of many of the borrowed pictures have, with the owners' permission, been added to the Archive. I owe a particular debt to my colleague Nuala la Vertue who has proved equal to every challenge in the hunt for elusive images.

History

Osney Abbey was one of the most striking architectural features of medieval Oxford with its huge stone buildings rising among the water meadows. It was founded in 1129 as an Augustinian priory by Robert d'Oilly the younger after his wife, Edith, heard magpies chattering in the Osney meadows and was persuaded by her chaplain that this required her to do something for the souls of the faithful in purgatory. Osney was raised to the rank of abbey in 1154 and became the wealthiest Oxfordshire monastery with a financial and banking business and property in more than 120 places. The great abbey church was rebuilt on a cruciform plan during the 13th century with two towers, a central one at the junction of the nave and transepts and a taller west tower. Substantial buildings for the abbot and canons were grouped around the church and the abbey precinct was extended to the south and west in the 13th century to enlarge and rationalise the site and improve the drainage. It is thought that the abbey mill was moved to the present site of Osney Mill at this time. Important Councils were held at Osney Abbey and Parliament met there in 1330; at Christmas in 1265, Henry III was entertained in the abbot's guest hall with "great revelling and mirth." The abbey features briefly as the employer of John the carpenter in one of Chaucer's *Canterbury Tales,* the bawdy Miller's Tale. In the story, John is cunningly sidelined while his pretty young wife, Alison, enjoys a night of passion with Nicholas, their student lodger. Osney Abbey was surrendered into the hands of Henry VIII in November 1539 and the abbey church briefly became the cathedral of the new Oxford Diocese in 1542. The site had practical disadvantages, however, and the last but one abbot, John Burton complained in 1537 that 'if he was to remain in such a damp place as Oseney his life would be shortened.' The bishopric was transferred to Christ Church in 1545 and much of the abbey was quarried away to provide ready cut building stone for the King's new foundation. The abbey's largest bell, Great Tom, was among the bells taken down from the west tower and removed to Christ Church. Many of the surviving buildings were destroyed during the Civil War and when Dr. Johnson was shown the remains in the 18th century, he remarked: "Sir, to look upon them fills me with indignation." Today, just a small portion of a 15th century waterside range survives above ground in Osney Marina; the main part of the abbey lay to the south and west of Osney Lane and Osney Cemetery occupies the site of the abbey church.

Transport has played a crucial role in the history of West Oxford and a prehistoric trackway probably crossed the Thames at North Hinksey before continuing north along the ridge towards Banbury. This route seems to have been followed by secondary Roman roads and would have involved fording a much broader river channel between the modern Hinksey and Bulstake streams. This crossing was called Oxenforde in 1352 and is one of many fords from which Oxford might have taken its name. There was a ferry at North Hinksey by 1370 and, because of this feature, the village was also known as Ferry Hinksey. In 1467, John Heyns the ferryman obtained permission from Osney Abbey to build a causeway from Botley Road to the ferry and this would have made the route passable for much of the year. John Leland, the antiquary, left Oxford by this route in about 1540 and, in June 1664, the Oxford historian, Anthony Wood, and two friends paid the ferryman threepence for rowing them across to North Hinksey. When Willow Walk was built in 1877-78 as a link between Oxford and a proposed estate above North Hinksey, the southern end of the old causeway was left as a pretty country walk. It remained popular until 1923 when Willow Walk was opened up as a public path and the ferry became redundant. Much of the ancient route became overgrown and impassable but it was restored in 1994 and is now sometimes called 'The Monks' Causeway'.

Botley Road is first recorded in about 1210 but it was only a seasonal footpath through the meadows until about 1530 when a causeway was built at the expense of John Claymond, President of Corpus Christi College. Narrow and poorly maintained, Botley Road was turnpiked in 1767 as part of an ambitious scheme to improve the road from Oxford to Eynsham. The causeway was widened and arched stone bridges were built over the many branches of the river Thames, giving Botley Road the alternative name, Seven Bridges Road; of those bridges, only St. Frideswide's Bridge still survives and that was widened in 1906. With the building of a new coach road up Cumnor Hill in the late 18th century, Botley Road became for the first time the main route from Oxford to Faringdon and the South-West. A turnpike gate was set up near Osney Bridge soon after 1766 and travellers had to pay a toll to use the improved road. The adjoining tollhouse was demolished in the later 1840s as the railway was driven through West Oxford but its successor, built in 1850, survives as the nucleus of the Old Gate House pub, now the White House. As the suburb of West Oxford expanded, the turnpike gate was moved to the west of Binsey Lane in 1868 and then to the foot of Cumnor Hill in 1877; three years later, the road ceased to be a turnpike.

Waterways were a practical alternative for moving materials around this low-lying area. The main navigation stream around Oxford, at least in the 17th and 18th centuries, followed Pot Stream from a point near the present railway bridge and went round Bulstake Stream to Four Streams, Walton Ford and Medley. Use of this roundabout route, which crossed Botley Road beside the modern Duke Street, was demonstrated in January 1686 when a boatman called Cock or Cox drowned in the Bulstake Stream and was later buried in St. Thomas's churchyard. With the building of Osney Lock in 1790, the present navigation stream was established on the old Osney millstream. Boats must have used the millstream to bring building materials and other heavy goods to Osney Abbey since Osney Bridge was known as Hythe Bridge in 1467; at the end of the 19th century, the area south-east of Osney Bridge was still known as Cannon Wharf. Throughout West Oxford, meadows were cut for hay every summer and, in areas best reached by water, punts would have conveyed the crop to the nearest dry land.

In Anglo-Saxon times, the first settlers in West Oxford looked for slightly higher ground in the watery landscape and the suffix —ey in the place names Binsey, Hinksey, Medley and Osney derives from the Old English word for an island. These areas could be virtually isolated by winter flooding and, writing about Binsey in 1872, Herbert Hurst remarked on 'the doleful aspect the place when it was hemmed in by floods.' Binsey is first recorded in 1122 but its origins are inextricably linked with the story of St Frideswide, Abbess of Oxford, who probably lived in the 8th century. According to legend, Frideswide fled to Binsey to escape her unwanted suitor, Algar, Prince of

Mercia, and he was blinded by a flash of lightning when he tried to seize her hand. She immediately felt sorry for him and St Margaret of Antioch appeared before her, telling her to strike her staff on the ground. Water gushed forth and, when Frideswide's attendants bathed Algar's eyes with it, his sight was miraculously restored. He also saw the error of his ways and went back to Oxford 'to lead a better and a wiser life.' Binsey church and the nearby St Margaret's Well became popular places of pilgrimage in medieval times and 'maimed and unsound folk' were reputedly cured by bathing in or drinking the water, hanging up their crutches as they left. It was claimed that nearby Seacourt had '24 inns and alehouses to entertain the multitude that came thither for the sake of this well' but archaeologists found no trace of this and the village was deserted by the late 14th century at a time when the popularity of the well was at its height. After the Reformation, St. Margaret's Well gradually lost its appeal and Anthony Wood, writing in the 1660s, remarked that 'now being overgrowne with nettles and other weeds, and harbouring froggs snails and vermin, [it] scarce owneth the name of a well.' Folk memories of the treacle, or healing, well survived, however, and credulous people were told about Binsey's treacle mines. In March 1863, Charles Dodgson, or Lewis Carroll, showed Alice Liddell and her sisters the remains of the well. The Rev T J Prout, vicar of Binsey between 1857 and 1891, restored the structure in 1874 and there is a story that he asked around the Senior Common Room at Christ Church for a suitable inscription; Lewis Carroll's helpful suggestion was 'Leave Well Alone'.

An imaginative reconstruction of Osney Abbey as it might have appeared in about 1520. H W Brewer's drawing, published in 1891, looks across the abbey millstream to the great abbey church and the distant keep of Oxford Castle. The spire of Rewley Abbey can be seen away to the left beyond the squat tower of St Thomas's Church. Osney Mill is in the foreground with a 15th century range to the right leading the eye towards the abbey fishponds.

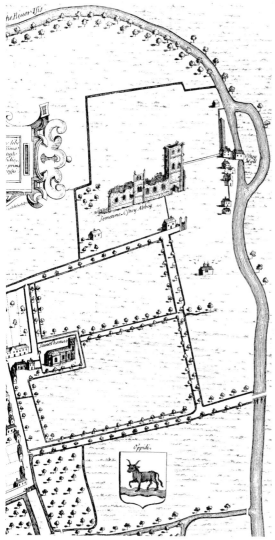

The site of Osney Abbey from Ralph Agas's bird's eye view map of Oxford in 1578. The abbey millstream flows south beneath Osney Bridge, past Osney Mill and the ruins of the abbey church. Botley causeway is visible just above the Oxford ox and St. Thomas's Church juts out into meadows at the end of High Street, St. Thomas's. The lane leading from Botley Road to Osney Mill was moved westwards to the site of the modern Mill Street in the late 1840s when the railway line was extended through West Oxford.

The west tower of Osney Abbey, an engraving by Wenceslas Hollar from a drawing by Hesketh in about 1640. This view from the south-east suggests that the tower was still complete when the ruins of the abbey church were destroyed in 1644 to complete the Civil War fortifications of Oxford.

The remains of Osney Abbey in 1720, two views by the artist Michael Burghers which show the 15th century waterside range that is visible on Agas's map. The lower view includes Osney Mill and, away to the left, the building which is now Osney Mill House. Burghers notes that the range marked 'd' seems 'to have been nothing but Out-houses'. A truncated section of this range, with a good queen post roof, still survives in Osney Marina.

Botley Road on 13 May 1781, looking east from Bulstake Bridge towards the distant towers and spires of the City. The Botley causeway had been turnpiked and widened in 1767 and it was also called the Seven Bridges Road because of the imposing arched bridges that carried the road across the many branches of the Thames. The Bulstake Stream flowing round to the Binsey Lane bridge (left) was the main navigation stream around Oxford at this time. (Bodl. Gough Maps 13)

A coach halts at the Botley Road tollgate and a lone horseman lingers on Osney Bridge. The tollhouse illustrated in this early 19th century painting was demolished in the late 1840s to make way for the railway.

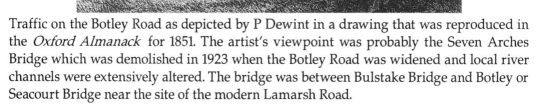

Traffic on the Botley Road as depicted by P Dewint in a drawing that was reproduced in the *Oxford Almanack* for 1851. The artist's viewpoint was probably the Seven Arches Bridge which was demolished in 1923 when the Botley Road was widened and local river channels were extensively altered. The bridge was between Bulstake Bridge and Botley or Seacourt Bridge near the site of the modern Lamarsh Road.

Osney Lock in 1822, an engraving by J and H S Storer. The lock was built by prisoners from Oxford Castle in 1790 and transformed the old abbey millstream into the main navigation channel through West Oxford. The old circuitous route along Pot Stream and the Bulstake Stream soon lapsed into picturesque decay.

An early 18th century view of St Margaret's Church, Binsey, from the south-east. After the Reformation most of the chaplains or curates at Binsey were Christ Church students who had very little to do with the place. The church, seen here with wooden shutters, was described by Anthony Wood as 'forlorne and naked' in the 1600s.

Benjamin Swete's house at Medley in the 18th century. An early 17th century verse commemorates Medley as a destination for river trips and an eating place. This house, built near Medley Manor Farm in about 1723, was a pub called the Cheese Cake in 1767. It was pulled down in about 1800.

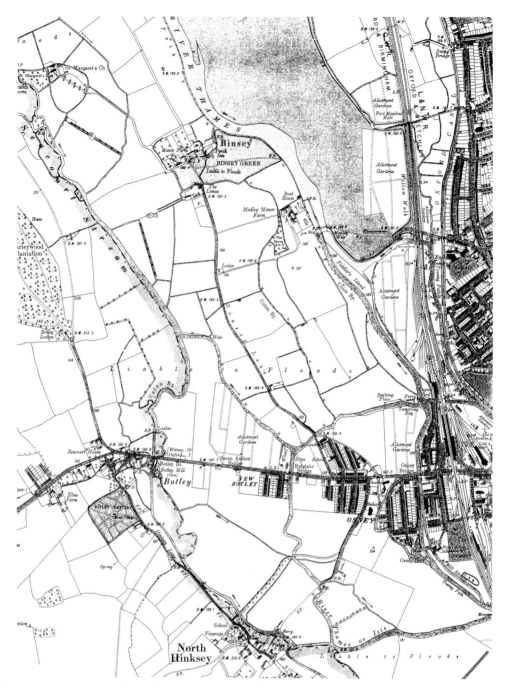

West Oxford in 1919. Branches of the River Thames, the railway and Botley Road are the major topographical features with streets of Victorian and Edwardian houses extending into low-lying meadows. South of Botley Road, the ancient route to North Hinksey has been partially upgraded but continues as a footpath to the ferry. Curving away from it, the unnamed Willow Walk was the major product of an unsuccessful attempt to build an ambitious housing estate above North Hinksey in the 1870s. Away to the north, Binsey and Medley remain quite rural in character, easily accessible for country walks in summer but isolated by floods in winter.

SECTION TWO

Railways

'A little railway town, more or less.' West Oxford was essentially a railway suburb, created in a few decades after the Great Western Railway extended its line through the area in the late 1840s and opened its passenger railway station in Botley Road in 1852. With the opening of the London and North Western Railway station in Park End Street in 1851 and the removal of the GWR goods station from Grandpont to Osney Lane in 1872, the concentration of local railway facilities in West Oxford was complete. Working long and irregular hours, railway employees found it convenient to live near the stations and, when few people had clocks and watches, they were also in range of the knocker-up who could wake them for early shifts. In 1871, nearly 30% of the occupied male population in West Oxford (107 out of 366) worked on the railways and, well into the 20th century, it seemed that 'you couldn't get a house down here ... because it was all railway'.

The two railway companies were employing 451 men and three women in Oxford by 1901, providing jobs for many local people and bringing other men to the City from more distant stations and depots. There was work not only for engine drivers, firemen and guards but also for porters, boilersmiths, fitters, clerks, cleaners, messengers, lighters-up and wheel tappers. From the mighty stationmaster to the humblest cleaner, everyone contributed to the running of the railway, 'God's Wonderful Railway' in the case of the GWR, and this common purpose built up a powerful sense of camaraderie. This feeling was only reinforced by the fact that many of these men lived nearby and met socially in local pubs and clubs. It was not always easy for outsiders to get jobs on the railways and, even in 1940, Leslie 'Dibber' Jones of Mill Street had to supply two references, one of them from a vicar, before he was accepted by the GWR as a temporary cleaner. Railway employment often passed down from generation to generation; both William Sawyer of Hill View Road and his son were porters on the GWR and Leslie Jones worked on the railway for 46 years between 1940 and 1986, just exceeding his father's service of 44½ years. Promotion never came easily and Leslie Jones was pleased to become a driver in 1956 after only 14 years as a fireman. He was later able to celebrate his status by taking the Night Worcester express down the Honeybourne bank at 100 m p h:
'We left Moreton in the Marsh and it used to be Evesham next stop. I said, 'Fill that firebox up with as much as you can get in there'. Luckily it was a good Castle, she steamed well. So we left there. I said, 'You won't have a chance to do any firing after I've left here'. I got round Aston Magna, there's a bend like that, and I opened her up; cor, we went down that bank so fast and we went through Honeybourne, she rolled and she just scraped the platform ... and I looked at my mate, he was as white as a sheet. Anyway, I shut the regulator and started braking and braking and braking and I thought, oh!, I'm not going to stop at Evesham and all of a sudden the brakes started to bind in and I put the brake in and I run into Evesham just as if I'd stop right for the water — perfect!'

After the War and following nationalization Oxford became a busy depot employing 100 sets of drivers and firemen. A messenger in the telegraph office at Oxford Station in the mid 1950s, Bob Allen remembers: 'We used to get a lot of trains in those days, fish trains from Hull, Grimsby, . . . every train that come to Oxford in those days — freight trains — was shunted as a rule, some was took off, some put on.'

The railway has been described as 'a noisy and obtrusive servant' and it has always been a prominent feature of West Oxford life. Houses on the east side of Mill Street back on to the railway and, in steam days, a pilot engine was always stationed on the line alongside their gardens to assist with shunting or to take the place of a failed locomotive. The Allen children scarcely noticed it but their mother was very much aware that 'when it used to let off steam all the smuts used to go all over her washing.' The sounds of shunting and the roar of passing trains, particularly at night, were heard throughout the area and station announcements wafted into homes in Abbey Road and Cripley Road. For youngsters like Brendan Carter the railway was a huge attraction and he and his friends would 'copy the trains' by taking down engine numbers or they would creep past the foreman's office window into the loco shed; 'cabbing it' or getting into the cab was their great ambition. Children put pennies on the line near the old Oxford North signal box and retrieved them after they had been crushed 'as big as Outspan oranges' by passing trains. The station complex provided opportunities for 'fox-hunting' as little gangs of boys evaded the ticket collectors and chased each other around the platforms and through the subway. Girls went along, too, and Edith Bartlett remembers being hauled off to the stationmaster's office for a ticking-off after she and her friends were caught drawing on advertisement hoardings. For employees, the railway became a part of their social life through sporting clubs and the Mutual Improvement Club; for railway families, it provided the occasional excursion and transport to a seaside holiday. The railway companies also supported the West Oxford Floral Fete on Botley Road recreation ground. A procession brought the Floral Queen to this annual show which included fairground entertainments, dancing and a produce show in a marquee; the local carpenter, Bill Day, was well-known for taking the prize 'for almost everything, carrots, onions, potatoes.'

Employees

Oxford's Great Western Railway football team in 1910/11. Seated in front of locomotive 3053, Sir Francis Drake, the players and officials are, from left to right: back row, M Brown, F Samsworth, F L Norris, F G Smith, I Weller, E Keefe, S W Saxton; middle row, A H Watts, G F Giles, C H Beesley, A Hunt (captain), A G Hall, F J Perkins, C G Collett; front row, F J Griffett, H R Cox. (LW)

Driver G Richardson (left) and fireman George Mace pose proudly on the running board of GWR locomotive 3515 in about 1910. The photograph was taken in the 'up' sidings to the north of Oxford station. (LW)

The staff at Oxford's GWR station in about 1925 photographed at the entrance to the 'down' platform. They are grouped around the seated figure of the stationmaster who, at this time, was Alfred Charles Foster.

Engine drivers grouped around locomotive 764, Sir Gareth, near the Oxford loco shed in 1937. They are, from left to right: back row, R Betts, C Parsons; middle row, Charlie Turner, R Field, K Hale, L Jackson, F Freestone, W Ponsford, J Sanwell; front row, W Boodell, C Woodley. An unidentified driver from the Southern Railway is standing on the ground. (LW)

Driver H J Bracey, cup in hand, and fireman, G W Padley, relax at Oxford before taking the 5.30 p.m. train to Paddington in January 1962. At the time, this was said to be the fastest steam train in Britain, covering the 63 miles non-stop in 60 minutes or less. (OCN)

A porter hauls a trolley of pigeon baskets along the platform in June 1955. Racing pigeon enthusiasts used the railways extensively until British Rail discontinued the service as uneconomical. (OCN)

Holidays for some mean work for others as a porter moves trunks and suitcases in July 1961. (OCN)

Everything but elephants; parcels piled high at Oxford station in December 1964.
(OCN)

Crates of cider being unloaded on to a Tuckwell's lorry at Oxford goods station in July
1957. (OCN)

Retirement in June 1958; Harold Spindlow (left), local representative of the District Operating Superintendent at Paddington, says goodbye to colleagues who had worked with him at Oxford before the First World War. The other men are, from left to right, J Miller, the Oxford stationmaster, P Thomas, F Trafford, E Brentnall and C Bloomfield. (OCN)

Jack Crook, a passenger guard at Oxford station, who was earning a basic £13 14s for a 42 hour week in January 1966 after 46 years service. As a guard he could be 'booking on or off duty at any time of the day or night' and he actually worked 48 hours a week, including rest days, in order to make up his money. (OCN)

The booking office on the 'up' platform or London-bound platform in 1962 with its racks of tickets for hundreds of destinations. The cheerful members of staff are J Hitchcock (left) and T Barrett. (LW)

Passengers

The 'up' platform at Oxford's GWR station in about 1905 with W H Smith's bookstall away to the right and a pointing-hand sign directing people to the stationmaster's office. This postcard view was sent by a disgruntled traveller who had nearly frozen at Guildford and now faced an hour and a half's delay at Oxford. (JD)

The 'down' side buildings of Oxford station are completely hidden behind drapes, flags and bunting to welcome King George VI and Queen Elizabeth on 24 October 1946. The King is standing with the Lord Lieutenant, Lord Bicester, and the City Macebearer during the playing of the National Anthem; the Queen stands to the left of the picture with the Town Clerk, Harry Plowman, and other civic dignitaries. Later in the day, there was embarrassment all round when the ceremonial key broke in the lock during the King's official opening of the New Bodleian Library. (MWO)

Girls from West Oxford Senior School pose happily for a group photograph on the platform before a trip to the Lake District in the 1950s. In the back row, from left to right, are Dorothy Barnsdale, Annetta Beasley, Ann Leach, Cynthia Hudson, — Ives, Mrs Todel, Shirley Rivers, Christine Jones, Elizabeth White, Ann Heppell, Janette Charlet, Joan Baigent and Jean Ives. The girls in the front row are Susan Sadler, Judith Melres, June Hudson, Janette Bushnell, —, and Enid Wells. (JDW)

Off for the summer holidays in July 1960. Dad and the children look out for the train while Mum keeps an eye on the family and their luggage. On the opposite platform, a poster advertising non-stop flights to New York seems to usher in a new era. (OCN)

A study in patience; intending passengers queue for tickets in the 'up' side booking office in September 1964. (OCN)

Unimpressed by a British Rail notice trumpeting new and better services for Oxford, passengers protest about the closure of facilities on the 'down' platform in February 1967. (OCN)

Demolition of the 'down' platform buildings in October 1971, looking down towards Botley Road and Cripley Road from a temporary bridge across the railway lines. The old GWR station was largely built of wood and, in 1911, Max Beerbohm, the author of *Zuleika Dobson*, remarked that, with its fading signals and grey eternal walls, it 'does yet whisper to the tourist the last enchantments of the Middle Ages.' (OCN)

Passengers preparing to board the London train at the newly rebuilt platform 1 in September 1971. The new station, built between 1970 and 1972, was only a temporary structure and the 'up' side facilities were replaced in 1989–1990. (OCN)

Platform 2 in June 1982 with newly arrived passengers making for the subway to the 'up' side; originally, the subway had also provided access to the nearby London, Midland and Scottish railway station. A footbridge replaced the subway in 1993. (OCN)

Churches and Schools

Churches

Apart from Binsey, most of West Oxford was historically a part of St Thomas's parish. As New Osney or Osney Town developed quickly in the 1850s, the Rev Thomas Chamberlain, vicar of St Thomas's, bought a site for a school-chapel at the corner of Bridge Street and South Street. This building was opened for worship on November 19th 1854 and a day school was certainly in being there by 1861. The New Road Baptist Church opened a small Sunday School in Osney Town in August 1857 and, as a result of overcrowding, a new building was erected in Bridge Street in 1864. Rivalry between the denominations probably encouraged the Rev Chamberlain and Christ Church, patrons of St Thomas's parish, in their determination to provide a permanent church to serve the growing district. Christ Church provided the site for St Frideswide's Church in 1870 and the architect, Samuel Sanders Teulon, was commissioned to design the building. Construction was delayed for a time by lack of funds and the church was opened on 10 April 1872 with its tower unfinished and the interior unadorned. A vicarage, designed by Harry Drinkwater, was added in 1876 but schemes for completing the church tower came to nothing.

St Frideswide's Church took on the High Anglican character of its mother church and the parish had a succession of remarkable vicars. The Rev George Kemp, vicar between 1872 and 1896, was a former Boxing Blue who is said to have floored an intruder in the belfry with a right to the chin. His successor, the Rev Augustus Miller had seven children and 'was frequently seen with a child on his shoulder (either his own or someone else's) like an amiable St Christopher'. Father Spence was a strong Anglo-Catholic who quarrelled with the Bishop of Oxford and became a Roman Catholic. The Rev G L Tremenheere was strongly opposed to alcohol and would not let male choir members go to the Hollybush after his services; instead, they went to the more discreetly placed Telegraph! His insistence that Gregorian plainsong was the only acceptable kind of church music drew unprintable comments from the choir which finally 'packed up and left en masse'. Tremenheere's successor, the Rev Charles Overy, was a keen archaeologist and a collector of antique and curious musical instruments. The Rev Arnold Mallinson was vicar of St Frideswide's from 1933 to 1976 and became, in addition, perpetual curate of Binsey in 1950. A numismatist and antiquarian, he was a first class preacher and an assiduous parish priest with a keen sense of fun. Henry Cummings has recalled how 'he gathered round him a nucleus of young people who met regularly for musical evenings – Arnold thumping out excerpts from D'Oyly Carte or one of the grand operas, Fred Stonham playing the violin, I endeavouring to sing'. June Warne remembers Shakespeare productions behind the church masterminded by Mallinson and the actor Willoughby Goddard. Of his many appearances in the press, the most memorable was perhaps his appeal in 1951 for a stuffed owl to clear bats out of Binsey church. The appeal attracted nation-wide attention and the vicarage was swamped by case after case of redundant owls.

The Baptist Sunday School in Bridge Street was disused by 1922 and many Non-Conformists and Low Church Anglicans attended places of worship in the city centre. The main alternative to St Frideswide's Church in West Oxford was the Railway Mission Hall built on the corner of Botley Road and Helen Road in 1904. When the foundation stone of this building was laid, T A Denny remarked: 'Railwaymen liked the company of other railwaymen, just as soldiers mixed with soldiers and sailors with sailors, and therefore it was needful that they should have a building in which to meet for worship.' The Mission Hall ran its own Sunday School and Miss Greaves, the head of West Oxford Infants' School, granted a holiday on 27 June 1924 because of the Mission's annual treat. She explained in the school log book: 'A great number of my children attend the Mission, and the Mothers take the little ones who do not attend.' Since 1953 the Mission Hall has been an Elim Pentecostal Church.

Flooding brings out the crowds in Bridge Street on 21 June 1903. The building topped by a cross on the corner of South Steet was Osney Town's first church, built through the efforts of the Rev Thomas Chamberlain, vicar of St Thomas's parish, in 1854. (Bodl. Minn Coll. 14/7B)

St Frideswide's Church in Botley Road in the 1900s when it was already partially hidden by horse chestnut trees. Designed by the architect, Samuel Sanders Teulon, and built between 1870 and 1872, the church was never completed because of a lack of funds. Its intended spire was never built, much of the external carving was left unfinished and the interior remained largely unadorned. (MPF)

The interior of St Frideswide's Church in about 1905, showing chairs, rather than more expensive pews, in the nave. The postcard view, marked with a cross to show 'where we generally sit', was sent by a woman called Dolly who had been staying in St Frideswide's vicarage and was having a jolly time; she expressed regrets that she was going to miss the Ascensiontide processions.

Botley Road in the 1900s, showing the Railway Mission Hall on the corner of Helen Road. The Mission Hall was built in 1904 to provide a building where railwaymen and their families could meet for worship. (JD)

St Frideswide's Church choir out-side the church porch in the early 1920s. (JL)

A wedding group on the steps of St Frideswide's Vicarage in about 1930. The happy couple are Nellie Hartwell from No. 20 Oatlands Road and Walter Neale. (JDW)

Palm Sunday procession at St Frideswide's Church in April 1962. Father Arnold Mallinson, vicar from 1933 to 1976, is on the right of the group with churchwarden Arthur Brightman, wearing a dark coat, in front of him. (OCN)

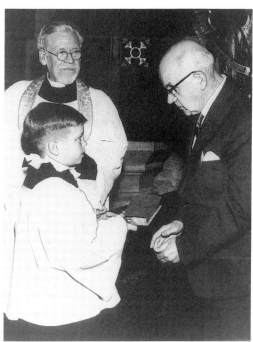

Jeremy Hogg and Graham Hartwell, two choirboys at St Frideswide's, collect money for the church from a passer-by, G D Denton, in June 1962. The 1930s bus shelter further along Botley Road was removed in 1973 when a bus bay was created on the site. (OCN)

Watched by the Rev Arnold Mallinson, St Frideswide's youngest choirboy, Garry Hogg, presents an English missal to Arthur Brightman in September 1963; Brightman had just completed 60 years of service to the church as churchwarden and accountant. He was a familiar West Oxford figure for many years, working as a clerk and later as accountant for W H Munsey Ltd at Osney Mill from 1903 until 1973 when he was nearly 90. (OCN)

Candidates for confirmation at Binsey Church in about 1964. Identified individuals are, from left to right, Graeme Hartwell, Mrs. Faulder, Mrs. Hartwell, Rev Arnold Mallinson, David Lewis, the Bishop of Oxford, Peggy Lewis (who later married the Rev Mallinson), −, −, −, −. (JDW)

Father Robert Sweeney, vicar of the parishes of St Frideswide, St Thomas and Binsey since 1979, joins builder, Ted Clarke, in placing a cross on top of the re-roofed tower of St Frideswide's Church in December 1985. The cross had formerly been above the apse and was relocated in this more prominent position to mark the completion of restoration work. (OCN)

The Power Station

From Roy Hoare: On the evening of Saturday, 18th June 1892, the new Oxford Electricity Company held a grand dinner at their new plant at Osney to inaugurate a supply of power to the City. Two hundred of the great and good assembled for a 'slap-up' meal, much of which was cooked on electrical appliances installed for the occasion. Music was provided by Herr Slapoffski and his band who played waltzes and operatic arias.

The Chairman, Mr Irving Courtney, after proposing the Health of Queen Victoria, went on with a lengthy description of the workings and intricacies of producing electricity, most of which went over the heads of the assembled. Sir Henry Acland, Professor Emeritus of Medicine, responded for the University, speaking of progress, comparing his 20-hour trip from Exeter as an undergraduate to the four hour journey of the day. Spencer Balfour, M.P. responded on behalf of the Government, concluding with: 'Might the City of Oxford always be worthy of the University and the University recognise the City'. Partway through the speeches the three generators had to be turned off so that the speakers could be heard, consequently the lighting went over to batteries and dimmed considerably.

Hillaire Belloc was inspired to verse by the event writing a piece that began:

'Descend, O Muse from thy mighty abode
To Osney on the Seven Bridges Road
For under Osney's solitary shade
The bulk of electric light is made....'

45 men were required to manage and operate the plant which produced 1,500 kw of power, (compare that with 2,000,000 kw generated Didcot). It was coal-fired and its sooty smoke would billow over Osney Island on an easterly wind, causing freshly washed clothes to be dirtied. On the upside, the 1 million gallon of warm water exhausted per hour from the boilers into the river provided a great swimming place for children (look out for the notice still there advertising this place to bathe). The clean-air Act of 1956 caused the plant to be oil-fired, after which the state of washing improved. The plant chugged on until March 1968 when it became obsolete. The buildings have since been used by the University's Turbo Machinery Research Group which are shortly to be relocated elsewhere and for museum storage.

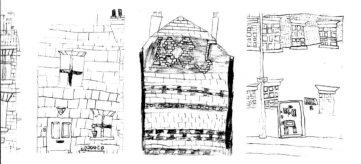

a very poignant reminder of what we all went through last year. Richard Thurston, outgoing chair of OIRA summarised the year as being dominated by the floods in which about 35 homes were affected and some neighbours had still not been able to return to their homes. He also reminded us of the successful Open Gardens day masterminded by Anna Truelove and the willows saga which took up much of last year when not occupied by the floods. Special thanks were given to Susanna Pressel and Colin Cook for their unstinting support of OIRA and to Pauline Martin for organising Oxclean on Osney.

OxClean

From Pauline Martin: **OxClean** is an Oxford Civic Society initiative, intended to draw attention to problems in and around Oxford that spoil the appearance of our streets and roadsides. **Spring Clean 2008**, over a weekend in March, was the first project and proved a big success, with 1,500 volunteers working in 99 different groups out doing their bit right across the city. Osney Island is not a problem area, except at its periphery eg the Botley Road area and the banks of Osney Stream, which our very own volunteer group cleaned up magnificently (thank you).

As a result of all the feedback from that event, **OxClean** is beginning to ask some searching questions on how to keep our city clean and tidy all year round, so that there is less to do when we spring clean next year. Anyone of my generation will remember a time when their mum routinely kept the front of the house, on to the street,

Schools

After St Frideswide's Church was built, the old school-chapel became St Frideswide's Infants' School and a new St Frideswide's Boys' and Girls' School opened next door on 15 August 1872. The schools theoretically had space for about 400 children but the boys had to play in the streets because there was no adequate playground. Having ignored criticism of the premises by successive HMIs (Her Majesty's Inspectors), managers launched an appeal for funds to build a new boys' school in 1901 and the new building in Helen Road opened in January 1905. The girls and infants were left with more space but the old buildings were impossibly decrepit; revealing some of the dangers, an HMI reported:

'At the end of the afternoon Session on April 23rd 1912, while the girls of the two lowest classes were being dismissed, one corner of a set of nine rafters gave way. The South window in the same room appears to be unstable. In wet weather the rain is driven through the crevices of this and the other windows of the room, and the roof leaks so badly that the rain water streams from one side of the room to the other.'

No funds were available for a new church school and West Oxford Council School was built in a former nursery garden in Ferry Hinksey Road, opening on 14 January 1914; the two-storey building housed the infants on the ground floor and the girls upstairs.

There was a strict regime in these schools, backed up by the threat of the slipper or ruler. The cane and even a rounder's bat were reserved for misbehaving boys and Mr Smedley, the 'cane-happy' head of St Frideswide's Boys' School, broke a wooden pointer over Ken Barrett's head in the 1940s. Miss Dymock, a teacher who transferred to West Oxford School when St Frideswide's closed in 1956, needed no such armoury. Bob Allen recalls: 'If you were bad or anything, she used to have you out and hold your hand and just slap you with her hand and she had massive hands, she really used to hurt.' Bill Stevens remembers that Mr Wainwright, sports teacher at St Frideswide's in the 1930s, 'was a dabster with the chalk, if you was nodding all of a sudden you had a smack on the face with a piece of chalk.' In June Warne's time, girls were put outside the door, made to face the cupboard or forced to stand in the corner wearing a dunce's hat.

Both boys' and girls' schools used a 'house' system to encourage good performance in academic work and sport. St Frideswide's had Raleigh, Nelson, Drake and Wolfe teams and Don Cross remembers that red stars had to outnumber black ones on a large chart at the end of school or the whole team would get detention. West Oxford Girls' School had Scott, Fry, Nightingale and Drake houses which competed against each other for sporting and academic trophies. Boys at St Frideswide's were expected to read and write by the age of eight and, according to Don Cross, 'you formed your characters properly not just scrawl them down like a piece of rubbish otherwise you did it all again.' Coming from St Thomas's to St Frideswide's at the age of 14 in 1937, Leslie Jones had to learn joined-up writing for the first time. Academic excellence was not always a priority, however, and Norman Bunning recalled that, in about 1930, 'if you could swim, run, play cricket, play football, he didn't care if you knew your ABC . . . you never learned a lot did you there?'

A broadening curriculum gave children more experience beyond the classroom. Infants from St Frideswide's School were first taken for country walks in 1905 and, with the encouragement of Colonel ffennell, classes from West Oxford Infants' School were visiting Wytham Woods by 1927. Sport took children on to the school playing field on Oatlands rec or to Tumbling Bay where, according to Renie Haffenden, 'we learned to swim on boxes on dry land.' Until the late 1930s, boys from St Frideswide's went to Merton Baths in Merton Street for swimming lessons during the winter; their teacher cycled there and back but they had to run! Gardening lessons took the boys to an allotment at Bulstake Close and, on occasions, to Harcourt Hill where the headmaster, Charles Wigg, had a large garden. Carpentry classes for boys and domestic science lessons for the girls involved a walk down to St Aldate's. Ethel Fowler's mother always made sure that she had clean clothes to wash; Mary Walton remembers eating most of her cookery work on the way home to Botley Road.

The Bishop of Oxford, Francis Paget, lays the foundation stone of St Frideswide's Boys' School in Helen Road on 8 July 1904.

Charles Hector Wigg (d. 1949) with his wife, Jessie, and children, Madge and Charles Elliott, at their home on Harcourt Hill in about 1914. Wigg was headmaster of St Frideswide's Boys' School for 36 years from 1896, retiring in 1932 with a bicycle, a cheque for £29 and a testimonial. He had a big garden and is said to have held some school gardening lessons there as a way of cultivating it. (JRJ)

Class 4 at St Frideswide's School with their teacher, Miss Dymock, in 1951. From left to right, the back row includes B Pill, Chris Broadway, F Jones, G Launchbury, G Floyd, R Stone, D Bedding, D Wooldridge, B Barnes, A Beesley. M White, R Gilby, M Woods, R Sansom, G Johns, P Chapfield, A Walton, R Skelcher, F Robbins are seated on the bench in the front row. (CB)

The St Frideswide's Boys' School football team in 1951/52 is posed against the school wall with the sports teacher, Mr Wood (standing left), and the headmaster, Mr Boyce. The boys, from left to right, are: back row, A Cox, L Palmer, T Day, R Titcombe, B Jones, P Harrison, J Beesley; front row, R Newport, G Potter, T Saunders, K Carter, P Finch, J Launchbury, R Rivers. (CB)

Class 1B at West Oxford Junior School in 1927. The boys would later go their separate ways to St Frideswide's Boys' School at the age of seven while the girls went off upstairs to complete their education in the Senior School. (PM)

Sewing class for the girls of Class V at West Oxford Senior School in about 1930. They are identified, from left to right, as follows: front row, Eileen Jones, −, Glenys Davis, Esme Howkins, Joan Richardson, −; second row, − (standing), Joan Kybyrd, −, −, Enid Pugh, −, −; third row, − (standing), Joan Carey, Avis Webb, −, Violet Gulliver, −, −; fourth row, − (standing), −, Joan Dingle, −, Dora Peart, −; standing at back, −, −, −, Iris Parsons, −.

Official group outside West Oxford Junior School in July 1935 when the Mayor, Ald. Pipkin (centre) and Sheriff (Ald. Somerton) (second from right) came to unveil a Silver Jubilee electric clock. Miss Lambourne, headmistress between 1925 and 1950, is standing to the right of the Mayor with the Canon John Stansfield, the former rector of St Ebbe's, behind her. In the background, there is a glimpse of the iron fence across the playground that separated juniors from seniors. (MJ)

A patriotic display of Union Jacks in West Oxford Junior School hall for the Coronation of King George VI and Queen Elizabeth in May 1937. (MJ)

Girls from West Oxford Senior School are dressed for a pageant on the Botley Road recreation ground in the late 1930s. The attractive pavilion behind them was designed in the City Engineer's Office by A Ablett who was the architect of some of the City's finest inter-War council houses.

West Oxford Senior School staff in 1948, a group photograph which coincidentally shows how the removal of railings for the war effort had left the playground undivided from Ferry Hinksey Road. The staff are, from left to right: back row, Miss Simpson, Miss Barr, Miss Hall; front row, Miss Shunn, Miss Hayes, Miss Benson. (GS)

Class 4 at West Oxford Senior School in 1948. The photograph shows, from left to right: back row, J Sansom, R Bellcourt, T Stevens, M Bridges, S Organ, V Grantham, J Baker, P Collett, J Baycock; middle row, M Bushnell, R Scarfe, J Parker, M Ellis, A Seath, G Sawyer, K Fisher, P Butcher, J Holton, G Butler, M Hill; front row, J Nelms, K Bricknell, J Carter, C Webb, E Green, Miss Shunn, M Edward, P Donehoe, R Lardner, L Gilbey, J Rouse. (GS)

Children gather proudly round a newly created school pond in the corner of West Oxford School playground in the 1950s. The school's outside toilets were behind the brick wall on the right and formed a regular source of complaint in the school log books. (MJ)

An afternoon off for West Oxford schoolchildren on 2 May 1968 when they walked down to the railway station to welcome the Queen on her visit to Oxford. (MJ)

Mel Summers, headmaster at West Oxford County Primary School from 1967 to 1981, helps 10 and 11 year olds with a project in Osney Town in January 1972. The children used trundle wheels, bits of paper and a clock to help them ascertain the speed of water flow in the River Thames. (OCN)

Watched with some merriment by other children, Andrew Timbs (7) tries his hand at skipping in West Oxford School playground in April 1987. The story arose out of a campaign to popularise skipping as a means of healthy exercise in schools. (OCN)

Dancing in the playground during an International Day at West Oxford School in July 1987. The dancers include, from left to right, Leah Tassell, Claire Clasper, —, Olivia Graham, —, Helen Broadway, —, —. (OCN)

The Lord Mayor comes to dinner; John Power enjoys a meal with West Oxford schoolchildren in December 1993. The school canteen, which originally served St Frideswide's Boys' School as well, was built in 1947. (OCN)

SECTION FOUR

On and Around the Botley Road

The low-lying meadows of West Oxford gained a new value with the coming of the railways and George Parsons Hester, the City's Town Clerk, bought the site of Osney Town by June 1851. In July, he launched development by offering '64 lots of various dimensions, suitable for gardens and building purposes.' Building went ahead swiftly, boosted by the demand for houses for railway families near the stations and, by the mid-1850s, much of Bridge Street was completed and there were several groups of houses in East Street and West Street. Osney Town housed 795 people in 141 inhabited houses by 1861 and regular floods which led to the area being nicknamed Frogs' Island did nothing to suppress demand; only one house was empty at the time of the 1871 census. Much of the western side of West Street was left as garden ground until the mid 1880s and the land beyond South Street, the Bridge Street extension, was only developed after 1891.

Encouraged by the success of Osney Town and the continued demand for artisan housing, Hester bought a more distant meadow beyond Bulstake Bridge and sold the first lots in New Botley or Bulstake Town in 1868. Barely raised above flood level, the development aroused much controversy and it was omitted from the City's main drainage scheme in the 1870s. A special pumping station had to be built on the Corporation Wharf in 1886 to pump the area's sewage to the main sewer at Osney. Public health concerns in no way delayed the development of New Botley and, by the mid-1880s, it was a suburb of 88 houses with a population of between 400 and 500.

As inheritors of the lands of Osney Abbey, Christ Church owned the area between the Great Western Railway line and the main River Thames. The college sold some extra land to the G W R in 1852, forcing Mill Street westwards to its present alignment, but showed no sense of urgency in developing the rest of the area. Finally, from the late 1860s, the area that became known as New Osney was gradually released for building on 80 year leases. The desirable Botley Road frontage was filled with tall three storey houses and Bridge House, the modern River Hotel, became the home of Thomas Henry Kingerlee. Kingerlee founded the largest building firm in Victorian and Edwardian Oxford and built many West Oxford houses from the late 1880s. Mill Street and new streets leading off it were filled with artisan housing, but the land nearest the river was reserved for business premises. The Oxford Electric Light Co., built its power station in Russell Street in 1892 and long-term residents remember Jones's nearby Osney Works, a mineral water factory which burned down in the 1940s. In 1877, John Galpin, a well-known Oxford speculator, agreed to build 68 semi-detached houses on the college's Cripley Meadow estate and the first houses were advertised as 'capitally suited for businessmen to whom time is an all-important object, half a minute would suffice to catch a train.' Middle class demand was just not there, however, and Kingerlee's completed Abbey Road and Cripley Road on a more modest basis in 1886.

By the 1890s there was virtually no land available for house building in West Oxford although there was a continued demand for local property from new residents and people wishing to upgrade to larger, more modern houses. Oatlands Meadow, owned by Morrell's Trustees, provided the solution and a first advertisement in October 1894 trumpeted the advantages of a site that was said to be within three minutes walk of the railway stations and the tram terminus in Park End Street. Thomas Gable, an Oxford publican, laid out Hill View Road in 1895, providing plots for others to develop. Gable died at the end of the year, however, and Kingerlee bought the unsold lots. The pace of development accelerated as Kingerlee's built the rest of Hill View Road and, in 1901, gained the City's approval for a building estate extending from Alexandra Road to Riverside Road. The firm also acquired land to the north of Botley Road and laid out Henry Road, Helen Road and the east side of Binsey Lane in 1902. House building progressed steadily on these estates but other developers were attracted by the prospect of cheap land with few restrictions on use. In Henry Road, the Co-op built a huge machine bakery on a site that had supposedly been reserved for a school; St Frideswide's Boys' School was slotted into Helen Road and a model laundry was erected in Binsey Lane. Harley Road and Riverside Road were only laid out in 1919 when the Savernake Glove Factory was built between them and house building in both streets was not completed until the late 1920s.

Oxford was a fast-growing City between the Wars but growth was focused on the motor industry and comparatively little development occurred in the low-lying Botley Road area. Businesses such as City Motors, William Baker's, Stephenson's and Hunt & Broadhurst were attracted to a main road location even if some local youngsters did their best to repel them. Norman Bunning remembers that 'when they built the garage we used to go along the scaffolding every night and they'd put the bricks up, you know, ready for the morning and we'd kick 'em all down.' Houses occupied other sites but no large estates were built. The City built just 20 council houses and temporary homes in West Oxford, four in front of the Corporation Wharf and the others in Ferry Hinksey Road. Private builders added a ribbon of semi-detached houses along the Botley Road between Binsey Lane and the City boundary by 1939. Street numbering was slow to reach the more distant properties and house names such as Kynance, Luxulyan, Verona or Malaga recalled or dreamed of idyllic summer holidays.

The modern semi remained rare in West Oxford and, for most residents, home continued to be a terraced house. In the older streets, most properties were entered directly from the black brick pavement but, from the late 1860s, it became usual to build terraced houses behind small front gardens. At No. 7 Hill View Road, Jill Wilson remembers 'Cast iron railings set on a little wall, a flowerbed beneath the wall and another in the centre; rope twist tiles lining the path to the front door. There was a shoe-scraper near the door' The decorative railings and gates were removed for scrap iron during the War; ironically, Kingerlee's, the firm responsible for putting up much of this ironwork, won the contract to take it all away. Most houses opened into a narrow passage or hallway leading to the front room and the living room. The front room or parlour was generally reserved for special occasions and most families preferred the central living room that was easier to heat by a coal fire or range. The warmth was only relative, however, and Gill Sawyer recalls that 'we used to have a fender that had two little seats on the side and we used to sit right in front of the fire, right up to the fire in those days.'

The scullery or kitchen lay beyond the living room and generally contained a range or cooker, a sink with a cold water tap and a copper for heating water or boiling up the laundry. Many households had inadequate cooking facilities and, in Osney Town, they paid a penny to have their Sunday dinners cooked in Woodward's bakery ovens. Between the Wars, coal-burning ranges gradually gave way to a gas cooker or, less commonly, to an electric cooker. At No. 7 Hill View Road, the electric cooker 'was very slow compared with modern cookers and the hotplates, ovens, etc., had to be put on long before cooking was to be started ... The oven was quite large but not on one occasion as large as a Christmas turkey my aunt got from Grimbly Hughes. 'Never mind Miss Mapleston, tell me the size of the oven and I'll shove his arse in for you,' said the cold-storeman (and he did and it fitted).' The copper in the kitchen was occasionally fitted with a pump to supply hot water in fitful spurts to an upstairs bath; most houses had no bathroom, however, and a tin bath hung outside the back door. Ann Allan remembers that 'Once a week on Sunday night we had the bath in front of the fire, in front of the open fire, filled it up with kettles and pans . . . I think the hardest job was carrying it out afterwards without slopping or spilling the water . . . My sister and I went in together, we were both quite small at the time.' The Carter family in Abbey Road varied this routine on occasions by going to the public baths in Paradise Square. A back door in the kitchen led to a yard which might house a mangle for washdays and, before fridges were available, a meat safe. Further down the yard most houses had an outside toilet, an arrangement that had been preferred because of health fears about sewer gas. Chilly places in winter, outside toilets became almost inaccessible after heavy falls of snow. Chamber pots in the bedroom provided night time relief and Brendan Carter has never forgotten the distasteful morning task of emptying the slops from up to 11 lodgers into a lidded bucket. Beyond each house a narrow garden, varying considerably in length, provided space for growing fruit, vegetables and flowers. Some people kept chickens in their gardens and sensitive children were always told that the chicken on their plate was a neighbour's bird; the Carters' pet chicken Betty was fortunate enough to escape the pot. Many households in New Botley kept pigs at the end of long gardens.

Upstairs, most houses had three bedrooms, the back bedroom over the kitchen being very small. Each room had a fireplace but these seem only to have been used in the event of illness and Ann Allan recalls rushing downstairs in winter to put on clothes warmed in front of the open door of the oven. Few West Oxford houses were built with an upstairs bathroom before the 1900s and, even then, bathroom meant just a bath and washbasin with a cold water supply. A toilet was fitted in the tiny bathroom of No. 7 Hill View Road soon after the War and the Misses Brakspear at No. 9 followed this example with some reluctance: "They found the idea quite distasteful but accepted they were getting on in years and some things just had to be faced. 'We only use it at night in bad weather of course, and then only for number ones.'"

These small houses were often filled to overcrowding. There were nine people in the Bunning family at No. 13 Earl Street in the 1920s: 'five of us in one room, three boys in one bed, two in another. Two sisters in the little room at the back, mother and father in the front.' After the War David Walker recalls that 15 members of the Rawlins family lived at No. 15 West Street and seven or eight Pearts at No. 44. There are stories, possibly apocryphal, of families sitting on the stairs to eat their meals because no room was large enough to accommodate them.

Flooding was a regular hazard in much of West Oxford and viewed almost as a fact of life. At Ted Coulling's shop in Botley Road, they received advance notice of floods from a man at the sewage pumping station opposite and quickly removed cheese, potatoes and other supplies from the floor of their semi-basement kitchen. Crates were placed on the floor and served as stepping stones to the toilet until they began to float; on one occasion, an unsuspecting commercial traveller on the way to the loo missed his footing on the crates and fell into the floodwater! Most householders had no flood warning. Frank Fowler 'went to work on the Sunday, I come back Sunday night; Ethel and her dad were sitting around the grate there and there was a cigarette packet floating round the grate with water.' Renie Haffenden came back from the cinema one day to find the saucepans floating in her kitchen. Mike Ferrett has vivid memories of his mother 'standing in the kitchen in her wellies just using the top of the gas cooker because the oven part was flooded.' Residents at the south end of Bridge Street spent a week living upstairs during the 1947 floods and, in an earlier incident when water was up to the front windows in Earl Street, Mr. Holliday at No. 10 took his pigs upstairs out of harm's way! People coped with all this because, as Renie Haffenden says, 'we were used to it, we didn't mind; in fact we was glad when it came every year because we used to go and mess about there.'

Except for Botley Road which was already becoming much busier between the Wars, the streets of West Oxford were remarkably peaceful until the 1960s. When Gill Sawyer was a girl in the 1930s there were no cars in Hill View Road and her father could turn his railway van round in an empty street when he came home for lunch; in Osney Town in the late 1940s, just three people owned cars. The streets were places in which to meet, talk and play, a crucial element in community life. As Gill Sawyer recalls, 'It was just a happy atmosphere. Didn't have to lock your doors or anything, you know, in those days, and families could just sit out on the walls in the summer and talk to one another and, you know, it was all friendly.'

West Oxford in April 1968, an aerial photograph that reveals many aspects of the area's history. Away to the right, the main channel of the River Thames since 1790 was probably built to serve the mill of Osney Abbey. The 17th and 18th century navigation channel via Pot Stream (bottom left) and Bulstake Stream (running from top left to top right) is visible beyond playing fields and allotments. Botley Road runs across the picture with Osney Town (middle right) and New Botley (top left) linked by a succession of short streets. Binsey Lane soon becomes rural again (top centre) and the ancient route to North or Ferry Hinksey is seen in its modern role as a distributor road for Osney Mead. The pre-industrial continuation of Ferry Hinksey Road (centre left) is masked by work on a scheme to preserve distant views of Oxford by putting electricity cables underground. Above this 'electricity road', the Victorian Willow Walk can be seen curving away from Ferry Hinksey Road like a railway embankment. Distinctive buildings, from left to right, include the former Ice Rink, West Oxford School, St Frideswide's Church and (centre right) Oxford Power Station. (OCN)

People line the pavement beside Botley Road railway bridge in August 1957, hoping perhaps that someone will risk driving through the summer flood. An advertisement on the bridge encouraged people to visit Lodge's on the corner of Mill Street; the hairdressing saloons were little cubicles approached through the shop. (OCN)

When the bridge was flooded, a level crossing was made available just to the south of the railway station. In this photograph, again dating from August 1957, traffic is flowing westward under the watchful eye of a railway official. (OCN)

The railway bridge from the west in the late 1940s with a prominent advertisement for Morris Garages Ltd., the Largest and Most Central of Oxford's garages. Sometimes described sardonically as Oxford's Arc de Triomphe, the bridge once famously proclaimed: 'Welcome to Oxford, the Home of Pressed Steel'.

A relaxing bus journey ends in disaster in September 1967 as the railway bridge claims another victim! In September 1939, evacuee children brought to safety in Oxford had their bus trapped under the bridge within minutes of their arrival. For decades until the bridge was rebuilt in 1979, low double decker buses had to be used on Botley Road services and notices on other types of buses requested passengers to warn the driver if he or she approached the bridge. A warning light system was eventually fitted on the bridge and at least one West Oxford resident had good reason to be grateful for it! (OCN)

New Osney and Osney Town

Mill Street in April 1963 when a lorry carrying a huge new tank for Oxford's power station was about to reverse its load into Russell Street. The power station was in the process of converting from coal to oil, bringing to an end decades of complaints about falling smuts in Osney. (OCN)

Botley Road, looking west from Mill Street towards Osney Bridge in the 1900s. The Old Gatehouse pub on the right, a tollhouse disused in 1868, is overshadowed by tall houses built in the 1870s. On the left, Miss Cross ran a little middle class school at No.7 for many years. Nearest Osney Bridge, Bridge House was the home of Thomas Henry Kingerlee (d.1929), a major Oxford builder who was Mayor in 1898 and 1911. In 1895, he stood unsuccessfully as Liberal candidate for the Oxford City parliamentary constituency. (JD)

Osney Bridge after its partial collapse on the morning of 2 December 1885. Cracks had appeared in the roadway shortly before the collapse which plunged at least four people into the river. Most were rescued but one 12 year old girl, Rhoda Miles from Swan Street, was drowned. While Oxford Local Board and Oxfordshire County Council argued about responsibility for rebuilding the structure, a temporary bridge for traffic was provided between East Street and Russell Street

Engineers pose proudly on the iron spans of the new Osney Bridge which was to open for traffic in December 1888. Much of the river flow had been diverted down other branches of the Thames to facilitate building operations. The building beyond the bridge was Galpin's timber yard and later became Kingerlee's carpentry workshop.

South Street in the floods of June 1903, looking west from the Waterman's Arms. Flooding in Osney Town was a regular event and the area was called Frogs' Island because the locals had to be virtually amphibious. On the right, beyond the punt and the Bridge Street junction, there is a glimpse of the old St Frideswide's School which was regularly closed because of flooding.

The south end of Bridge Street in March 1947 when Osney island, like other low-lying Thames-side communities, suffered serious flooding after a very hard winter. (RH)

Council workmen build a walkway through the floods outside No. 56 Bridge Street in January 1959. These gang-planks were ideal for local children who enjoyed playing on them when nobody was looking; Mike Ferrett remembers being pushed off the planks on his way to school and earning a welcome day off. (OCN)

Mrs H M Gaisford of No. 26 Bridge Street prepares to mop up the flooding in her kitchen in December 1954. Gas cookers on legs sometimes remained above the water line but, at No. 115 Botley Road, Mary Walton remembers occasions when her mother was unable to use the oven or even the top. (OCN)

Granny Rolfe sits in the back yard of No. 62 Bridge Street in the 1920s. The cupboard behind her, roofed to keep the sun off, was a meat safe, designed to keep food cool in the days before refrigeration. (RH)

A military vehicle uses a pontoon bridge to cross the Thames between East Street and Russell Street in March 1943. This structure, following the course of the temporary Osney Bridge in the 1880s, was built as part of the large-scale Spartan Exercise when troops from 'Southland' advanced on Eastern Command forces representing a German-held 'Eastland'. (H27933 Courtesy of the Imperial War Museum, London.)

East Street and the Oxford Power Station in the late 1940s. The Thames towpath was still a workaday feature without trees and narrow boats delivered coal to the power station by means of a hopper which descended from the gantry over the river. Local people cursed the smuts from the power station that fell on their washing when the wind was in the wrong direction; on the other hand, hot water pumped into the river provided year round swimming and opportunities for hair washing!

Peggy Inness and her niece Pauline pose happily on a car's rear bumper outside No. 41 West Street in about 1950. On the opposite side of the street a large gateway to former business premises forms a break in the row of mid-nineteenth century terraced houses. (PM)

Mr and Mrs Phipps outside their house at No. 17 Bridge Street in October 1977. The photograph was taken to illustrate traditional sash windows that were fast becoming a rare feature in changing Osney Town; the residents' parking sign indicated another modern transformation since, just 30 years before, only two or three people on the island had owned cars. (OCN)

Botley Road opposite St Frideswide's Church in January 1973. The installation of a bus bay and the removal of the old bus shelter were a response to the growth of traffic along an increasingly busy road. (OCN)

Ferry Hinksey Road to Bulstake Bridge

Mary O'Donaghue, a Ferry Hinksey Road resident, protests about excessive traffic in the road in June 1985. Once a footpath and then a country lane, the street became a residential road at the Botley Road end between the 1890s and the 1920s. Since the 1960s, it has also become a busy link road between the growing Osney Mead Industrial Estate and the rest of Oxford. (OCN)

Albert Bayliss and his wife at No. 111 Ferry Hinksey Road in May 1980. Their home was one of a group of wooden huts that had, according to local tradition, been built to house soldiers returning from the First World War. In fact, the huts were erected as temporary council houses in the mid-1920s and their survival for nearly 60 years was little short of remarkable. (OCN)

A quieter pace of life in Botley Road in about 1910, looking east from the junction with Helen Road and Alexandra Road. A woman cyclist heads for Botley and a horse and cart goes into town. On the left, a milkman stands beside his churn and young street trees flourish on a wide pavement; away to the right, the Osney Arms is receiving a delivery.

Harold Brown has Hill View Road to himself as he cycles towards Botley Road in about 1910. The Hill View estate was laid out on part of Oatlands Meadow in 1895 and, before other developments got in the way, it had fine views towards Harcourt Hill and Cumnor Hill. (KC)

Gill Sawyer in her pram outside No. 24 Hill View Road in about 1935. Most of the houses in the street were built to a similar design by the local builder, T H Kingerlee and the front gardens had ornamental gates and railings; ironically, Kingerlee's won the contract to remove all this ironwork for scrap during the Second World War. (GS)

The daily struggle for parking spaces in modern Hill View Road, seen from the bay window of No. 9 in September 1989. The view includes the Osney Arms pub on the corner of Botley Road and, in the distance, Osney Mews which had just replaced the Co-op dairy in Henry Road.

No. 2 Helen Road in about 1910, showing the proud occupants, Clive and Bertha Beesley, and another couple. Helen Road and Henry Road were laid out by Thomas Henry Kingerlee in 1902 and he named them after two of his children. (JL)

Unofficial evacuees outside No. 10 Alexandra Road in the early 1940s. These men were just two of the evacuees taken in by the Hartwell family during the War. Others included a Maltese chemist and two Jewish women, Hetty and Fay Shuter, who ran a shop selling children's clothes next to Warland's. (JDW)

A woman stands in front of the air raid shelters which stood on Oatlands Road Recreation Ground during the Second World War. Local children enjoyed playing in and around these shelters but, when the sirens went off, most people took refuge in their homes. West Oxford School made use of the shelters during air raid alerts and drills but the headmistress, Miss Lambourne, complained that they were dark and wet; sometimes, flooding made it impossible even to reach them.

Alexandra Road in the snow in about 1947. Kingerlee had submitted plans to build this road in 1901 and suggested the name Queen Alexandra Road as a tribute to Edward VII's consort; the City Council was not convinced that it was a sufficient tribute and made him drop the word Queen! (JDW)

Bill Hartwell on his motorbike outside No. 20 Oatlands Road in about 1926. (JDW)

Riverside Road in February 1986, with 1920s semi-detached houses on the left built by James Tyler. The British Telecom Depot on the right, demolished in 1992, was built in 1919 as a factory for the Savernake Glove Co.; glove making was envisaged as a major local employer but the factory only remained in business until 1931. The former Ice Rink is visible at the end of the street.

Botley Road in April 1903, looking east towards the Red House, No. 92 Botley Road, on the corner of Binsey Lane. Trees have been planted on rudimentary pavements but there was still countryside to left and right. Oatlands Road was laid out in 1910 but development ceased during the First World War; for some years, much of Oatlands Meadow was a weed- and rubble-strewn eyesore hidden behind hoardings. On the left, allotments occupied land behind the hedges until the late 1920s. (Bodl. Minn Coll. 5/24A)

Watched by the local bobby, surveyors question four motorists in Botley Road during a traffic census in 1949. The Ministry of Transport paid half the cost of this 'origin' and 'destination' survey.

The Wood Farm bus makes use of the Botley Road bus lane opposite Bishop's depository in December 1973. The bus lane was an early product of the City Council's new *Balanced Transport Policy*, introduced to speed buses through the traffic on an increasingly congested road. (OCN)

A pedestrian strides purposefully across the new part of Bulstake Bridge during the widening of Botley Road between Binsey Lane and Botley village in 1923–24. The improvement was a joint project between Oxford City Council and Berkshire County Council and its main inspiration was the need to provide work for the unemployed.

New Botley to the City boundary

Botley Road, looking west from Duke Street in about 1910. This area, known as New Botley or unofficially as Royalty Square, was developed on a piece of freehold land from 1868 and it remained detached from expanding West Oxford until after the First World War. The off licence on the corner of Duke Street flourished for many years on local and passing trade and other houses on the main road were converted into shops as the Botley Road became busier.

Duke Street in July 1967, looking down towards King George's Field. This street of varied houses, erected by a number of builders over some 20 years, formerly ended at a boarded fence which mischievous local lads vaulted over to escape the local policeman. In 1935, however, St John's College gave the meadow behind the fence to the City and it became a recreation ground to mark the Silver Jubilee of King George V.

Botley Road in the early 1920s, looking towards the City centre from Botley Bridge. A sign just beyond the fence warns motorists of a 10 m.p.h. speed limit that had been introduced in 1910. Boys from Earl Street could still play football in Botley Road at this time and Joan Bates, recalling many walks to Seacourt farm, was surprised to see more than the odd vehicle.

Workmen employed on the Botley Road improvement scheme take a break from pile-driving near Botley Bridge in 1924. The work at this point involved the demolition of Botley Mill and substantial alterations to the river channel as well as the rebuilding of Botley Bridge.

Traffic in the Botley Road in February 1977 with the Carterton bus outside Barclay's garage. The semi-detached houses towards the left of the picture were part of a ribbon of housing and commercial development that filled the gap between New Botley and the City boundary in the 1920s and 1930s. Barclay's had taken over the former Co-op bakery in 1974. (OCN)

John Patten, M.P. for Oxford West and Abingdon, leads protesters challenging Robert Maxwell to explain his plans for Nos. 199–215 Botley Road in November 1991; Steve Stuart, holding both placard and cycle helmet, is one of the other campaigners. A Maxwell company purchased the site of Hunt and Broadhurst Ltd., manufacturing stationers, behind these houses and offered owners of the so-called 'Maxwell Houses' large sums of money in an attempt to create a vast development site. There was fierce opposition to the loss of housing and the properties were later restored as part of a retail warehouse development. (OCN)

West Oxford Countryside

Until the mid-19th century the area west of St Thomas's was entirely rural and visitors to Oxford were advised to go and enjoy the sight of undergraduates riding to hounds along the Botley road. The West Oxford countryside has been much eroded since then and drivers inching their way along Botley Road today could be forgiven for thinking that the whole area is now buried under bricks, tarmac and concrete. In fact, however, the West Oxford suburb is a narrow ribbon of development that has been raised above the Thames flood plain and clings to Botley Road as if to a lifeline. The Osney Mead industrial estate massively extended the built-up area in the 1960s but West Oxford is still predominantly green and Binsey village retains a remarkable air of remoteness.

Botley Road itself retained a rural aspect until it was widened and improved in 1923–24. As a child in about 1920, Joan Bates would walk from her home in Hythe Bridge Street to Seacourt Farm in Botley on Saturday mornings and 'it would be remarkable if one horse and cart passed me; absolutely silent except for the whirr of the telegraph poles . . ., completely quiet, tall hedges on both sides . . . The road was very narrow of course . . ., it really was countrified.' Cattle were driven to market down Botley Road on Wednesdays and sheep were washed in the river to the north west of Osney Bridge. At this date, the Corporation Wharf on the site of Prestwich Place represented the only development west of Binsey Lane on the north side of Botley Road; on the south side, there were no houses between Oatlands Road and New Botley. Beyond Earl Street countryside resumed and Bill Stevens remembers a pond near the site of Lamarsh Road and 'Old' Johnny Cox, an odd-job man who lived nearby in a caravan and chased away trespassing boys. Percy Soanes worked in one of the fields making wooden hurdles for sheep pens. Development soon changed all this but rural links were maintained as carriers from North Berkshire brought grocery orders from local farms to Ted Coulling's shop at No. 115 Botley Road and collected provisions as they went home in the evenings. Mr Coulling himself travelled twice daily to a farm in Cumnor to milk his cows and look after his pigs and chickens. The countryside still came to Botley Road every week until the 1960s as cattle were driven from the Oxpens cattle market to the Co-op slaughterhouse opposite Ferry Hinksey Road. Animals sometimes escaped from the slaughterhouse and Brendan Carter recalls a cow 'dancing up the road and the traffic was all held up for a while before they got it back.'

As Botley Road became busier it became necessary to seek out true countryside elsewhere. At the end of Ferry Hinksey Road, Payne's Field was a huge open space named after the Oxford coal merchant who leased it to provide grazing and hay for his horses. More recently, many West Oxford residents remember the local farmer, Bill Grant, living in a caravan opposite the Co-op garage in Ferry Hinksey Road and keeping his animals in the field. Ethel Fowler picked snakeshead fritillaries in Payne's Field as a child in about 1930 and boys from Osney Town would take sausages and a frying pan and spend all day over there; some lads at least made up for their trespassing by helping to stack the hay at harvest time. In September, Payne's Field was the scene of West Oxford's own fair at the end of St Giles' Fair and, in winter, it sometimes became an open air ice rink. The Osney Mead industrial estate took over this green space but branches of the river Thames still flow lazily through the crucial belt of meadowland which separates Oxford from North Hinksey.

Gerard Manley Hopkins wrote passionately about the felling of Binsey poplars in 1879, but the rural character of Binsey and Medley has proved more resilient than he would have dared to hope. Much of the land between the River Thames and the Western bypass is still farmed and the farms at Binsey and Medley both maintain herds of cattle. Medley Manor Farm was entirely given over to grass when Charles Gee took it over in 1958 and, although he has since ploughed up about 30 acres, he has kept much of the ancient meadowland with ridge and furrow: 'I'm a bit old-fashioned perhaps but I like the permanent pasture because the cattle seem to do quite well.' The Medley Ram Fair was held annually in a field off Binsey Lane until the early 1960s and, in the later years at least, some of the sheep were brought from a distance. The lots were penned up with wooden hurdles, probably made nearby by the hurdle-maker, Percy Soanes, who had transferred his business from Botley Road to one of the yards in Binsey Lane by 1934. Mr Soanes's hurdles were once sent as far afield as Scotland but the increasing use of wire or electric fencing was cutting demand for his traditional product before he retired in about 1970. Another Binsey Lane yard was a pig farm after the War. Sheep are no longer reared at Medley following trouble with stray dogs but Charles Gee turned proximity to the City to advantage in 1979 when he began to grow 'Pick Your Own' fruit and vegetables. Medley Manor Farm must be one the few PYOs where pickers on bikes are almost as numerous as those in cars.

Inspired by the growth of rowing and yachting on the Thames above Medley, two rival Oxford families, the Bossoms and the Beesleys, opened boatyards there in the later 19th century. Initially, boat hiring was their main business and both firms hired out boats to the Oxford University Sailing Club between 1884 and 1923. In the 1950s, Bossom's began to build and repair boats and to provide moorings for privately owned cruisers. John Ballance and Derek Bennett of Bossom's successfully developed fibreglass 'Alpha' racing dinghies for the University Yacht Club in 1958 and, at the time of the Falklands War in 1982, the firm supplied radomes to protect the radar equipment of the R.A.F.'s Harrier jump jets. Current output includes glass fibre sailing dinghies, classic launches, military boats and, since the recent takeover of Frank Collar's business, wooden oars.

Fewer than 30 people lived in Binsey in 1974 as against 63 in 1921. The falling numbers are due in part to reduced employment on local farms and the disappearance of the old subsistence economy when many Binsey householders kept flocks of geese. In addition, Binsey's picturesque 18th or 19th century cottages had few modern conveniences and water had to be fetched from wells or a communal standpipe until 1958. At the same time, no new housing has been built to attract escapees from the urban rat-race which seems so near and yet so far away. The aviation pioneer, Geoffrey de Havilland (1882–1965), spent much of his boyhood at Medley Manor Farm with his grandfather, Ald. Jason Saunders. Towards the end of his life, he returned to Medley expecting everything to have changed beyond recognition; instead, he was surprised and delighted to find many links with the past. Binsey was successfully defended from proposed gravel workings and the building of a reservoir in the late 1950s when the western bypass was being planned. Today, traffic noise is sometimes intrusive but the physical fabric and the surroundings of Binsey and Medley are still intact; north of the Perch, the successors of Gerard Manley Hopkins' fallen poplars still grace the river bank.

The Thames towpath looking north from the footbridge across the Sheepwash Channel in about 1962. Seemingly remote and yet within sight and sound of the busy railway, this spot was known to local children as 'The Farm'. It served as an unofficial playground and as a place for Guy Fawkes' Night bonfires. The ferry to Tumbling Bay crossed the river at this point and generations of local people walked or cycled here on their way to the bathing place. (OCN)

Navigating Medley Weir in May 1925. The weir keeper has removed the paddles and rymers from the weir and swung back the beam and catwalk to let a boat travel downstream. One of the last 'flash locks' on the Thames, Medley Weir was removed by the Thames Conservancy in 1928.

Hard times at Medley Weir cottage in February 1974. Anne Winkworth, resident at the cottage for 40 years, shovels coal into a coal scuttle during the worst floods that she could remember. (OCN)

Medley in about 1880 when rival boat builders and hirers, William Bossom and G Beesley, faced each other across the River Thames. In Victorian times, with the growth of nearby North Oxford, Medley became a popular starting-point for river outings to Godstow and beyond. The Oxford University Sailing Club held its first race above Medley in May 1884 and Medley Sailing Club was established in 1937 in a shed belonging to Bossom's.

Taking the dogs for a walk at Medley boat station in January 1960. During the floods, Richard Horton needs a punt to reach dry land on Port Meadow. (OCN)

Cattle stand contentedly in the pond outside the Perch at Binsey in the 1900s. Manor Farm is visible in the background. The thatched Perch dates back to the 17th century as a building but there is no record that it was a pub until 1831. By 1842, it was described as 'well-known' and it has remained a popular destination for visitors from Oxford.

Mrs Lund and her daughter collect water from Binsey's communal tap in July 1958. This standpipe brought mains water to Binsey and was the first stage in supplying each house with a mains supply. Before this, villagers had to rely on their own wells or on water pumped by a windmill from a deep well. (OCN)

Mrs Phyllis Venables, the licensee of the Perch, inspects the fencing of Binsey Green in July 1960. On fine summer weekends, between 80 and 100 cars had been driving across the Green to park by the river and landowners, Christ Church, fenced the area off to restrict access; despite her smile, Mrs Venables feared loss of business. (OCN)

Alderman Jason Saunders (d.1911) and his wife outside Medley Manor Farm in about 1900. As well as running the farm, Saunders had a successful haulage and removals business in Oxford and was Mayor of the City in 1876. He was the grandfather of Sir Geoffrey de Havilland and crucially gave the aviation pioneer £1000 to build his first aeroplane.

A man lingers on the ancient causeway to Ferry or North Hinksey in about 1900. After Willow Walk was opened up for pedestrians in 1923, this route lost its purpose and it gradually became almost impassable; happily, it was restored to use in 1994.

The Mayoral party uses the ferry to cross the Hinksey Stream while beating the bounds of the City on 17 August 1892. Identified individuals include the Chief Constable, Supt Head, with his back to the camera, and Jack Bossom, wearing a cap and the uniform of a university waterman. The Mayor's sergeant, Mr Beckwith, is carrying the City Mace. A footbridge now provides a safer link between West Oxford and North Hinksey at this point.

A young explorer and his dog on the Willow Walk footbridge in the 1920s. For West Oxford youngsters this route provided a launch pad for many adventures, a day's swimming or paddling perhaps at the nearby Ducks and Pool or more distant flower picking or birds' nesting on the hills above North Hinksey.

Sheep and horses graze peacefully in Osney Mead in the early 1960s when the Oxford Preservation Trust tried unsuccessfully to have the area included in the Oxford Green Belt. The obelisk in the foreground commemorates 21 year old Edgar George Wilson who drowned nearby after rescuing two boys from the river on 15 June 1889. (OCN)

Farmer Bill Grant ferrying hay and feed to his flock of pregnant ewes marooned in a field off Botley Road in March 1982. Until recent years he kept ewes and their young lambs in a field off Ferry Hinksey Road that was easily supervised. The sights and sounds of Spring contrasted with a huge electricity pylon and the nearby industrial estate. (OCN)

A family boating party on the Bulstake Stream in late April 1987; Peter Graham is in the bows and Olivia (left) and Ros Graham in the stern. Apparently in the heart of the countryside, this is in fact a precious wild life corridor with the Osney Mead industrial estate just one field away to the left.

A surprisingly rural view of West Oxford, looking west towards Wytham Hill from Abbey Road in about 1975. The allotments in Twenty Pound Meadow, and Botley Road Recreation Ground beyond them, were threatened by a Botley Road relief road scheme in the 1970s. That plan was defeated but the future of West Oxford's surviving countryside often seems precarious.

Business

The development of West Oxford created a demand for goods and services in each area and led to the establishment of many local shops. In Osney Town between the Wars there were four shops in Bridge Street, Woodward's the baker's at No. 34, Hammond's general shop at No. 69 and small shops run by Granny Morris (No. 71) and Granny Hudson (No. 76); Eric Organ ran another general store at No. 24 West Street. Ethel Fowler remembers Granny Morris as 'a little old lady and . . . nearly blind. What you went in for you used to help yourself to and give her the money and . . . everyone was quite honest with her. She never used to sell much, reels of cotton and odds and ends.' Renie Haffenden recalls a huge tub of lard or dripping in the shop. Granny Hudson's shop sold almost everything and later became Kernahan's. Woodward's was founded in 1882 at No. 69 and moved across the road in 1904 after building a bakery on the site of its former stable. In the 1930s, the firm made about 2,000 loaves on weekdays and about 2,800 at weekends and it supplied the local market as well as Littlemore Hospital, many Oxford pubs and other establishments. Until about 1959, door to door deliveries were made by a horse and cart driven by a local character, Albert Hunt; the firm's horse, Tom, enjoyed a pint or two of beer on his rounds! Woodward's shop was only open for a few hours daily for local bread sales and Hammond's business, later run by the Birds, was the main general store on the island. The Birds opened on weekdays from 8 a.m. to 8 p.m. and on Sundays as well to attract local custom but the shop closed down in 1976. Mike and Pat Ferrett developed Woodward's into a general shop and it flourished for a time, particularly on its evening trade, but the opening of large supermarkets with extended opening hours forced Osney Town's last shop to close in December 1997. In 1998, the bakery was still busy, making about 700 loaves on weekdays and 1,400 at the weekends for shops, delicatessens, colleges and pubs.

Elsewhere in the suburb local people had an extensive choice of shops offering basic necessities and more specialist services. Residents growing up in Mill Street after the War remember Lodge's and Hudson's at the top of the street and Manning's further down on the corner of Barrett Street. Lodge's was a sweet shop which also supplied 1s 6d blocks of ice cream to go with special puddings; beyond the shop, there was Audrey's, a ladies hairdresser's in a little room, and a barber's shop with three chairs. On the opposite corner, Hudson's was a newsagent's and general store, remembered for its huge £sd cash till, its tempting tins of loose biscuits and its large slicing machine for cooked meat. Brendan Carter has good reason to remember the bare wooden floor, 'going in there with sixpence to buy a Daily Sketch and I dropped it between the floorboards and she wouldn't let me have the paper.' Manning's did a good trade from the nearby railway hostel and Ann Allan recalls that the shop was 'particularly renowned for its penny lollies which he made himself. I think it was just squash that he put in ice cream trays.' Cripley Road had Mrs Webb's general shop on the corner of Cripley Place. West of Ferry Hinksey Road, Botley Road became a neighbourhood shopping centre with a post office, a chemist, a newsagent, several grocers and butchers, a fish shop, a confectioner's, a shoe repairer's and a draper's. Joan Bates recalls Thomas's grocer's shop on the west corner of Henry Road in the 1920s which proclaimed that it was 'A Noted House for Bacon'. Mr Skelcher from Medley Manor farm ran a grocer's shop on the corner of Hill View Road and had a milk round in the area; his shop later became a Co-op grocery store where you left your order and a delivery boy brought it round on foot or by bike. The Co-op was a local supermarket in its later years and its closure in 1979 was much regretted. June Warne has fond memories of Sybil Cox's grocery shop at No. 69 Botley Road as 'a real typical sort of local shop where everybody met, everybody talked there and if anyone didn't turn up you always knew if someone was ill or bad.' In today's very different circumstances, Eggs Eggsetera, established in about 1972, serves a similar role as a local food store and a chance meeting place for residents. Most food retailers have abandoned the area, but the chemist's shop and post office survive on their original sites. Specialist firms include Oxford Ironmongery and Warlands cycle shop which took over a former draper's shop on the corner of Alexandra Road in 1937.

New Botley had its own parade of shops extending west along Botley Road from the corner of Duke Street. In the 1930s, this included Coulling's grocer's shop and off licence, Cambrey the butcher, Humm's sweet shop, Jenkins the dairyman, the Maces' ladies hairdressing business and George Messenger's general shop. Coulling's, at what is now No. 115 Botley Road, sold virtually everything, including beer, wine and spirits, groceries, fruit and vegetables, sweets, tobacco, milk and cheese, bacon, paraffin, bundles of wood for lighting coal fires and maize and corn to feed the local chickens. Before refrigerated units were acquired in the 1940s, the shop had daily deliveries of fresh food and bacon, for example, was kept in the cool basement kitchen under a muslin cover. Mary Walton recalls that 'people used to just come in and buy what they wanted for that meal; if they wanted cheese or they had bacon for breakfast or eggs for breakfast and that, they used to just come and buy them and they'd get them fresh you see.' Bill Stevens worked for Harold Cambrey in the late 1930s and did deliveries by bicycle to the new housing estates in Botley. On one occasion he was sent off on his bike to pick up some meat from the G W R goods station in St Thomas's: 'He only dropped 125 lb. top piece and rump in the basket! Of course, I couldn't get off because, I mean, if I'd got off it would just have tipped up on the front and broken on the floor . . . I had to ride all the way from there, round the corner, under the station arch, over that bridge, the river bridge, and down here and stop outside the shop.' Cambrey moved to the new Elms Parade in Botley in 1939 and the shop became a branch of White's the greengrocer's after the War. Humm's business was later Kumbak's sweet shop which became well-known all over Oxford; the young Don Chapman visited it every Saturday afternoon to 'spend' his post-war sweet ration.

One local industry, flour milling, pre-dated the growth of West Oxford by hundreds of years. Osney Mill was established on a branch of the River Thames in the 12th century and has probably been on the present site since the early to mid 13th century. The mill outlived Osney Abbey and, if plans by William Stumpe, a Malmesbury clothier, had come to anything, it might have been at the heart of a large clothmaking industry in the 1540s. Gunpowder was made in Osney Mill during the Civil War but flour was its usual product and it was enlarged in the later 19th century to become a steel roller mill. W H Munsey came to Osney in the 1890s and his grandson, Bill, remembers that imported grain was brought to the mill by barge and later by rail. Between 25 and 30 people were employed at the mill and the flour was delivered to bakeries within a 30 mile radius. A serious fire in 1946 ended milling at Osney but Bill Munsey still lives in Osney Mill House where he was born and he continues to run Clark's flour mill at Wantage.

As the Victorian suburb developed, its proximity to the river attracted a number of employers. The Oxford Electric Light Co. chose Russell Street as the site for its power station in 1890 because large quantities of water were needed to cool the steam condensers and a riverside location meant that barges could deliver coal directly into the works. The power was switched on for the first time on 18 June 1892 and inspired Hilaire Belloc to poetry:

> Descend, O Muse, from thy divine abode,
> To Osney, on the Seven Bridges Road;
> For under Osney's solitary shade
> The bulk of the Electric Light is made.
> Here are the works; from hence the current flows
> Which (so the Company's prospectus goes)
> Can furnish to Subscribers hour by hour
> No less than sixteen thousand candle power,
> All at a thousand volts. (It is essential
> To keep the current at this potential
> In spite of the considerable expense.)
> The energy developed represents,
> Expressed in foot-tons, the united forces
> Of fifteen elephants and forty horses ...

The power station initially generated electricity for lighting the Oxford colleges, public buildings and a few grander houses. A few street lights in central Oxford were converted to electricity but gas lighting remained cheaper and new housing estates in the 1930s were still being lit by gas. The Osney power station was enlarged as demand increased and it generated electricity for the National Grid until March 1968. It was a noisy and polluting neighbour and Ethel Fowler remembers: 'If the wind was in the right direction you used to get all this sludge from the chimney on your washing ... well, you used to get it in the yard, you used to sweep that up. It was annoying when you'd done a nice lot of washing and you got all smut bits over it.' The power station had its advantages, however, and locals used the hot water returned to the river for hair washing and all the year round swimming. Lumps of coal would fall into the river while barges were delivering and, as Renie Haffenden recalls, children 'used to go dive at night, pick the coal up and bring it and put it on their mum's fire.'

The river attracted Kingerlee's, the Oxford building firm, to its Abbey Road yard in the mid-1880s and, when Ken Charlwood joined the firm in 1939, timber was still being off-loaded from barges north of Osney Bridge and delivered across the towpath. The firm's stone yard off Mill Street was also handy for delivery by water. Established in Banbury by Thomas Henry Kingerlee in 1868, the firm moved to Oxford in the 1880s and was soon Oxford's largest builder, employing between 200 and 300 men. It had its own brickworks in North Oxford and a builders' merchant's business in Queen Street. Kingerlee's was heavily involved in speculative house building in the City and submitted plans for nearly 600 houses, many of them in West Oxford, between 1886 and 1914. From the beginning, the firm also tendered for building contracts and it later concentrated on this kind of work. Notable Kingerlee buildings in Oxford include

Rivermead Hospital (1886), the Apollo Theatre (1933–4), St Luke's Church, Cowley (1938) and St Mary's Church, Bayswater (1958). The firm has also worked extensively for Oxford City Council, schools, colleges and hospitals and for the former Pressed Steel Co., at Cowley. Many employees on Kingerlee sites are sub-contracted but the firm has retained its own highly skilled workforce. Francis Harris worked for the company as a joiner for 50 years between 1941 and 1991, beginning his apprenticeship at Abbey Road by making padded boxes for the Spitfire radiators produced by Osberton Radiators. The joinery workshop moved to Lamarsh Road in 1960 when Kingerlee's concentrated all its activities on a site that it had leased as a builder's yard in the 1930s.

The Thames Conservancy opened a maintenance yard beside Osney Lock in the 1910s and employed about 20 or 30 men there between the Wars. Frank Fowler recalls a high boarded fence behind the Bridge Street houses which prevented local residents from taking advantage of the yard's coal store. At the end of the working day, employees caused a brief rush in Bridge Street: 'They used to ... be sitting on the saddles of their bicycles at five minutes to five [waiting] for the whistle to go at five o'clock and then you used to get out of the way because a whole stream of them used to come out of there.'

Comparatively cheap freehold land drew a number of other businesses to West Oxford. In 1904, the Oxford and District Co-operative Society Ltd. built a large machine bakery and employees' houses on a site bounded by Henry Road, Botley Road and the Osney ditch. The site later included offices and a slaughterhouse that continued to kill cattle, sheep and pigs from local farms and markets until the 1960s. In Osney Town, Mike Ferrett remembers the slaughterman, Harry Saunders, 'coming home at lunchtime in his brown overalls all covered in blood and gore he was a horrible sight.' The Co-op built a new bakery at the far end of Botley Road in 1954 and the old Henry Road bakery was transformed into the City's largest dairy. The society opened a transport depot in Ferry Hinksey Road before the War and Frank Fowler began work there as a fitter in 1946, opting for the job because he would get £4 16s 0d for a 48 hour week, two shillings more than he had been offered anywhere else. He went on to become transport manager with a fleet of 456 vehicles and looked after the Co-op's Botley Road garage which opened opposite the bakery in the 1960s. The Co-op became a major landowner in West Oxford and tried unsuccessfully to launch superstore developments on its properties, the first in Botley Road in 1977 and the second in Osney Mead in 1980.

Two well-known local firms, Hunt & Broadhurst Ltd. and Alden Press, occupied premises in Binsey Lane that had been built in about 1905 for the Oxford Model Laundry Ltd. Hunt & Broadhurst's, the educational stationers, outgrew its first home in Paradise Square and moved to Binsey Lane in 1925. Renie Haffenden was only the fourth female employee when she went to work there in 1929 and she earned 7s 6d a week for wire stitching and glueing exercise books by hand. She recalls that, after about two years, 'Old Mr Broadhurst came along and he said, 'I see your work's improving, Renie' and I always remember he wrote on the table 3d ... 'You'll get an extra threepence in your wages this week'.' Hunt & Broadhurst moved to a purpose-built factory, the Ideal Works, along Botley Road in 1935 and Gwen Ilsley started working there on printing work for the government in 1945. She was the firm's 48th employee and saw numbers rise to 400 as the works expanded considerably after the War. Alden Press moved from Cornmarket Street to Binsey Lane in 1926, sharing the premises with Hunt & Broadhurst's until 1935 and then occupying the whole site. Some rebuilding was done but John Alden recalls fairly ramshackle buildings and uneven floors over which employees had to drag heavy pallets of paper measuring up to 64 inches by 44 inches. His first office was 'a cubby hole in the corner of an entrance hall. I used to hear the huge machine through the wall pumping out, woof, woof, woof, woof, because you had this vast weight of the bed of the machine reciprocating back and forth.' Jonathan Cape Ltd. bought a substantial interest in the firm in 1932 to ensure priority treatment and Alden's printed the first general edition of T E Lawrence's *The Seven Pillars of Wisdom* for Cape's in 1935. The book made huge profits for Cape's but not for Alden's and, in 1953, John Alden described the link between the firms as 'once a helping hand, now a dead one.' The Alden family bought out Cape's in 1959 and diversified into printing scientific journals, becoming major printers for Blackwell Scientific Publications and a number of learned societies. Increasingly cramped at Binsey Lane, Alden's moved to a large open plan factory in Osney Mead in 1965 and it now has 250 employees in Oxford and at a typesetting branch in Northampton.

The Botley Road area provided space for several other commercial ventures between the Wars. The Savernake Glove Co. built a large glove factory on a site between Harley Road and Riverside Road in 1919, but the premises had become a Post Office maintenance depot by 1932. City Motors, founded in Gloucester Street in 1919, opened its first branch garage in Botley Road in 1922. During World War II, the garage became a miniature arsenal, repairing fighter aircraft and rebuilding or maintaining military vehicles and equipment; many servicemen were also trained there as fitters. As car ownership increased City Motors opened a new Botley Road showroom in 1959 but, in 1978, the firm sold the site to Hartwell's after opening a new garage near the Woodstock Road roundabout. Stephenson's, founded as coal merchants in Jericho in 1876, opened a large builders' merchant's showroom and yard at Nos. 185–195 Botley Road in September 1935. In the post war years, the firm pioneered Do It Yourself locally and it opened the first major oil-fired central heating showroom in Oxford in September 1959. Other businesses finding sites on the south side of Botley Road included William Baker & Co. Ltd., which established a furniture factory making everything from sectional bookcases to coffins. Varsity Express Motors Ltd. built a garage at Nos. 169–171 in 1929 and this was later occupied by United Counties and then by South Midland. The mineral water manufacturers, Corona, also had premises at the corner of Lamarsh Road.

The short-lived Oxford Ice Rink, opened in 1930, was the only major business among the houses on the north side of Botley Road. Its successor, the Majestic Cinema, gave Bill Stevens a job as uniformed page boy and his duties included checking tickets, showing people to their seats and cleaning the snooker tables. A member of staff had to fetch change from a bank at Carfax and sometimes borrowed a bike to do the job more quickly. Disaster struck one day when another local lad, Chris Cox, 'put the money on the back . . . on the carrier, sort of job. Coming down the road he got under the station arch and the bag busted and all the coppers and that were flying about in the street.' After that incident, the change was always collected by bus! The Majestic closed in 1940 but Frank Cooper Ltd. converted the building into a new Victoria Works in 1949, moving from their old premises in Park End Street. Cooper's employed 150 people at the factory, including a quality care supervisor who had to confess, in 1955, that she didn't like marmalade. Local residents and passers-by on the Botley Road were constantly aware of the 'whiff of Seville oranges' until the factory was closed in 1967 and the production of Oxford marmalade moved to Wantage and then to Paisley. For a time Oxford Instruments housed its electronic and cryogenic production facilities in the building but the furniture retailers MFI turned the place into a furniture showroom in 1971.

A converted ice rink did not necessarily provide the most practical retail environment and, in 1985, MFI won an appeal against the City Council's refusal, on traffic grounds, to allow a new warehouse on the site. This decision set off a chain of developments that have transformed parts of Botley Road into an unofficial retail park. Stephenson's redeveloped their extensive site as three large warehouses during 1987 and sold out to Jewson's in January 1988. Hunt & Broadhurst's plans for a warehouse, garden centre and car park on their site were turned down in 1986, but the firm was taken over by Pergamon Holdings Ltd., one of Robert Maxwell's companies in 1988. The business was sold on to Fine Art Developments in the following year and was relocated to Bradford. Pergamon retained the site and set out to improve access to it by purchasing Nos. 199–215 Botley Road for demolition. Householders were offered far more than the market rate for their properties but one family stood out against the deal. A lively campaign, which included a sleep-in in cardboard boxes, helped to save the so-called Maxwell houses but the Hunt & Broadhurst factory was pulled down in 1991 and three more warehouses occupied the site. Such developments have threatened to submerge West Oxford in a slow-moving tide of traffic.

Green Belt policies have largely confined postwar development in the area to the existing built-up areas. Efforts to have Hinksey Meadow zoned for industry in October 1961 were successfully resisted by the City Council because the site was seen as 'a buffer between Botley Road and Hinksey.' Relief road schemes to the north and south of Botley Road have been vigorously opposed, partly because they would intrude into the Green Belt. Osney Mead or Payne's Field was, however, specifically excluded from the Green Belt and, in the City's Development Plan of 1955, it was zoned for industrial purposes. Building on this land had been foreshadowed before the War by the Co-op's transport depot in Ferry Hinksey Road; the local fruit and vegetable wholesalers, Harold Hicks & Son, also built a distribution warehouse there in 1939. Hartwell's built an oil depot behind Ferry Hinksey Road in the 1950s and Boffin's opened a new bakery off what is now called Electric Avenue in 1955. In January 1961 the City Council approved an outline application by University College to develop Osney Mead 'for [the] relocation of badly sited industries in the City of Oxford.' Development went ahead in 1963–64 and the first firms to take advantage of the spacious estate included Knowles & Son, Symm & Co., Alden Press and Oxford Instruments. Oxford Mail and Times Ltd., shoehorned into an old furniture warehouse in New Inn Hall Street, looked at other options before moving to purpose-built premises in Osney Mead in February 1972. Don Chapman, well-known for his Anthony Wood column in the *Oxford Mail,* helped to market this move to readers by organising a mead-making competition. After two specially designed Osney Mead trophies had been broken in the post, the winner received a third one of a more robust design. When the move actually took place, Anthony Wood pretended to make the journey by punt from Folly Bridge before hitching a lift on a passing coal lorry. In fact, Don Chapman simply drove in from Eynsham on the Monday morning and turned right into Ferry Hinksey Road, a junction that still needed no traffic lights. By 1979, however, 33 firms were based at Osney Mead and, as traffic levels have increased, there have been frequent calls for a relief road from the estate to Botley Road or to the Southern Bypass. It is all a far cry from the days when Payne's Field was quiet meadowland and a place for informal recreation.

Shops

Reginald Hammond's shop and off licence at No. 69 Bridge Street, Osney Town, in the 1930s. Between 1958 and 1976 Mr and Mrs Bird ran this shop, opening from 8 a.m. to 8 p.m. on weekdays and on Sundays as well. (VO)

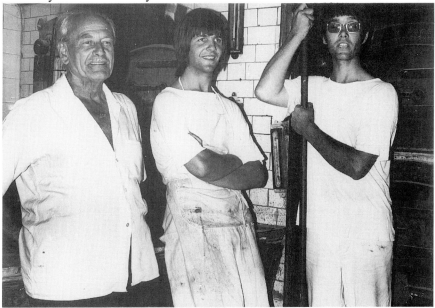

Percy Woodward (left) with Paul Ferrett (centre) and his brother, Mike, in Woodward's Bridge Street bakery in about 1972. Percy was the grandson of William Woodward who had founded the business at No. 69 Bridge Street back in 1882; the bakery moved across the road to No. 35 in 1904 and its Edwardian ovens remained in service until 1976. (MPF)

Bread from Osney; Woodward's baker's van, driven by Albert Hunt and hauled by Tom the horse, trots through Jericho in September 1947. 'On Mondays the horse would go to the top of the street [Bridge Street] and turn left because he knew he had to go to Botley that day and on Tuesday he'd go right and he'd stop outside all the doors'. (MPF)

Woodward's shop at No. 35 Bridge Street, just before its closure in December 1997; the photograph includes, from left to right, Pat Ferrett, Muriel Casey and Pam Cox. The shop's owners, Pat and Mike Ferrett, no longer found the business viable: 'we used to catch most people coming home from work. They used to pop in because they'd forgotten something. Now I think they go straight to the supermarkets.'

Employees of Morland's Brewery at Abingdon make sure that supplies continue to get through to the Waterman's Arms in Osney Town despite the flooding in November 1954. (OCN)

Bill Bowell and his son, Ian, find a new use for a pushchair while delivering newspapers in flooded Bridge Street in December 1979. (OCN)

John Simpson, West Oxford milkman for the Co-op since 1951, needs
wellington boots to deliver pints to
Ted Barrett of No. 44 Bridge Street
in December 1979. (OCN)

Mr and Mrs. Baxter stand proudly outside their boot and shoe shop at No. 25 Botley
Road in about 1916. The display of good leather was clearly seen as a selling point. (JD)

Baxter's business reborn in 1922 as Haines's wet fish shop. While two assistants hog the limelight with the horse and cart, Ernest Haines is content to peer out through the shop window. Haines's was well-known for its delicious fish and chips. (JL)

George and Mary Walton promise the Best Shoe Repairs at their shop at No. 33 Botley Road in the 1950s. With the rising price of leather, the cost of replacing soles and heels rose to 2s 6d a pair for ladies' shoes and 3s 6d a pair for men's shoes. Mary's only recollection of shoplifting was an occasion when someone went off with an empty display tin of Kiwi shoe polish.(MW)

A display of Armour's Veribest corned beef and ox tongue in Coulling's shop window at No. 115 Botley Road in 1936 or 1937. This temporary promotion won the business a carrier bike which helped with the delivery of produce from this well-stocked grocer's shop. One of the council houses built beside the Corporation Wharf in Botley Road is reflected in the shop window.(MW)

The employees and delivery vehicles of W Jenkins' Botley Meadow Dairy, photographed in about 1910 in a field opposite New Botley; two of Mr Jenkins' milkers are visible in the background. His shop was just across the road at what is now No. 123 Botley Road.

Local firms

Group outside Osney Mill in about 1911; the young man with a natty bow tie is Ellis Munsey whose nephew, Bill Munsey, still lives at the Mill House in the background. The Foden Steam Wagons helped W H Munsey, Ltd. to supply flour to small bakeries and other outlets within a 30 mile radius of Oxford. (BM)

Miss S Belcher (left) and Mrs N. Bradbury are the cheerful bearers of some of the 80,000 hot cross buns which the Cadena Bakery expected to make at Easter 1960. Bill Munsey had provided the bakery with a site near Osney Mill on the condition that the firm used his flour, an arrangement that worked well until the firm was taken over and closed down. (OCN)

Passers by look on with interest as Thames Conservancy frogman, Peter Madden, surfaces beside Osney Weir after cutting old wooden piles from the bottom of the river in April 1973. The Thames Conservancy has been a long-term employer in Osney Town and older residents in Bridge Street recall a mini rush hour of cyclists at the end of the working day. (OCN)

Invitation to Alderman Thomas Green and his wife to attend the opening of Oxford's Electric Lighting Station in Russell Street on 18 June 1892. The wholesale use of University and College coats of arms on the invitation was perhaps an attempt to give added status to the new source of power. The works, located by the River Thames, are illustrated below the General Manager's name.

The directors and employees of the Oxford Electricity Co. Ltd. pose for a group photograph at the Osney power station in 1924. In 1931, Oxford City Council took over the right to supply electricity within much of the city and it managed the power station until the electricity industry was nationalised in 1948.

'Deafie' Galloway working on boiler No. 3 at the Osney power station in about 1955. (OCN)

Women workers at the Co-op dairy's bottling plant in October 1954. The plant was then one of the largest in the industry with a capacity of around 9,000 gallons a day. (OCN)

Unloading milk churns into the Oxford and District Co-operative Society's Henry Road dairy in November 1960. The dairy was a noisy neighbour in an otherwise residential street but perhaps less troublesome than the Co-op bakery which had occupied the building until the 1950s. One long-term resident recalls that bakery workers pushed bins around the tiled floors all night and regaled the street with a repertoire of songs that always began with 'Abide with me' and finished with 'To be a farmer's boy'. (OCN)

A smart delivery team poses outside the premises of the Oxford Model Laundry Ltd. in Binsey Lane in about 1910. The laundry was built near the Binsey Lane bridge in about 1905 and was managed by Frederick Smith and his wife; it remained in business until about 1920. Alden Press and Hunt & Broadhurst, Ltd. later occupied and adapted these buildings.

E A Wymer (left), managing director of Frank Cooper's, shows Monty Woodhouse, M.P. for Oxford, a huge vat of Oxford Marmalade at the firm's Botley Road premises in March 1961. Frank Cooper's moved from Park End Street to the former Ice Rink and Majestic Cinema in 1949 and older residents can still remember the 'whiff of Seville oranges' wafting around West Oxford. Production at Botley Road ceased in March 1967. (OCN)

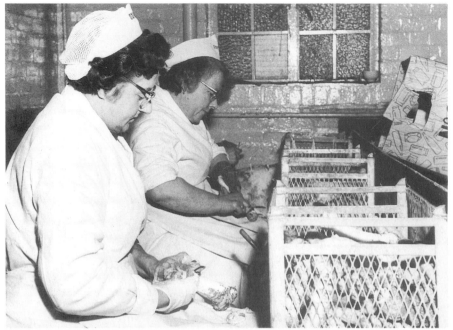

Employees of Frank Cooper's peel horseradishes in March 1961 as the first stage in the manufacture of the firm's famous sauce. Local people were keen to grow horseradish on their allotments because Cooper's would pay up to a guinea (£1.05) a pound for the bridging root; years later, horseradish still grows everywhere on West Oxford allotments. (OCN)

'Fill her up, please'; a City Motors employee at the Botley Road garage gazes intently at the indicator on the petrol pump in the 1930s. City Motors, founded in 1919, opened their first branch in Botley Road in 1922 and the premises were used for all sorts of war work between 1939 and 1945.

Tom Bridges, managing director of City Motors, gives a hairdryer to a lucky motorist, Major L G Harber of Cumnor Hill, at the Botley Road garage in September 1959. Chiltern Motor Holdings Ltd. became the parent company of City Motors in 1968 and sold these premises to Hartwell's in 1978. (OCN)

Francis Harris using the overhead planer at T H Kingerlee's joinery shop in Lamarsh Road in May 1991. Mr Harris joined Kingerlee's in Abbey Road as an apprentice joiner in 1941 and, apart from war service, stayed with the firm until his retirement in 1991. One of his first tasks was to help make padded boxes for the Spitfire radiators that were being manufactured by Osberton Radiators in North Oxford. (FH)

Three Kingerlee's employees, Tony White, Bill Freeman and Norman Wright, cheer the receipt of long service awards in December 1989. Tony White had worked for the firm for 50 years. (OCN)

Stephenson's proudly display their Botley Road premises and their fleet of delivery vehicles in 1937. Founded as coal merchants in Jericho in 1876, Stephenson & Co. (Oxford) Ltd. opened as builders' merchants in Botley Road in 1935. Don Chapman remembers going there with his father in a pony and trap in the 1940s to buy asbestos sheets; on the way home, a bus passed them and 'this poor little pony took fright, kicked up its heels and all those sheets of priceless asbestos shattered into bits. We had to bring them back and piece them together because we couldn't afford any more.' (OCN)

Strikers picketing the Lamarsh Road entrance to Stephenson's during a pay dispute in June 1984. The photograph shows the size of Stephenson's premises and, in 1987, the firm secured planning permission to redevelop the site as three retail warehouses, intending to occupy one of them itself. In 1988, however, the business was sold to Jewson's. (OCN)

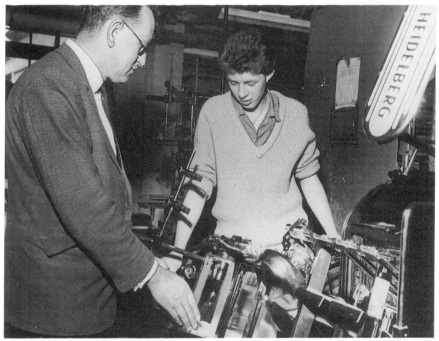

J Godwin, printing department overseer at Hunt & Broadhurst Ltd., shows an apprentice, P Emery, how to load an automatic printing machine in May 1961. Hunt & Broadhurst moved to Botley Road from premises in Binsey Lane in 1935 and became important manufacturers of exercise books, notebooks and stationery products, employing 400 people in the 1950s. (OCN)

Finnish paper suppliers are shown round Hunt & Broadhurst Ltd. by John Broadhurst (second from left) and Keith Lloyd (far right) in about 1980. The firm tried unsuccessfully to redevelop its site from 1983 and was taken over by Pergamon Holdings Ltd. in 1988; the business was sold on to Fine Art Developments in 1989 and relocated to Bradford, leaving the site to be cleared for retail warehouses. (OCN)

A glimpse of a much quieter Botley from the scaffolding as the Co-op bakery in Botley Road takes shape in May 1954. The bakery closed down in 1972. (OCN)

The Fiat service centre opened by J D Barclay Ltd. in the former Co-op bakery premises in 1974. The men admiring the new facility are, from left to right, Edward Cox, director, and Peter Lee, director and general manager of J D Barclay Ltd., with Castrol's Trevor Grove. (OCN)

Drivers and lorries outside the premises of Hicks & Son (Oxford) Ltd. in June 1966. Hicks, the wholesale greengrocers, opened a warehouse in Ferry Hinksey Road before the War and their premises became the Oxford equivalent of Covent Garden market, sending out about 20 vans of fruit and vegetables every morning to places within a 40 mile radius. (OCN)

Tankers belonging to Hartwell's Oils (Oxford) Ltd. filling up for the day's work at the firm's Ferry Hinksey Road depot in September 1959. (OCN)

Almost 100 members of staff from the Alden Press are photographed outside the firm's Binsey Lane works in 1952. All but three of the employees have been identified. (JA)

F Kimber (left) shows Mrs Cicely Alden and Ralph Lane, company chairman, one of the Alden Press's printing machines at the opening of the firm's premises at Osney Mead in October 1965. The new building included an open plan factory with space for expansion and a two-storey office block that could easily have a third floor added; this element of future-proofing was soon justified by the subsequent development of the firm. (JA)

Bob Davies continues typesetting by the light of emergency generators at Alden Press during the Three Day Week in 1974. (JA)

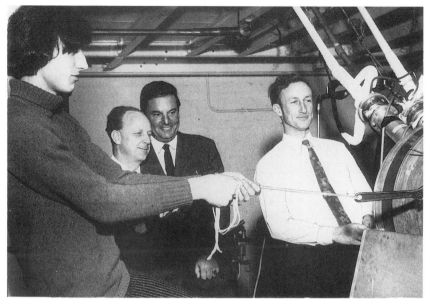

Victor Regoczy (left) demonstrates the pulling power of a superconductive quadrupole magnet that was being completed by Oxford Instruments in January 1970; watching the experiment, from left to right, are Don Cornish, Dr. Alfred Asner and Dr. John Williams. The magnet was one of the world's most advanced magnets and had been built over nearly two years in the unlikely surroundings of Frank Cooper's disused Victoria Works in Botley Road. (OCN)

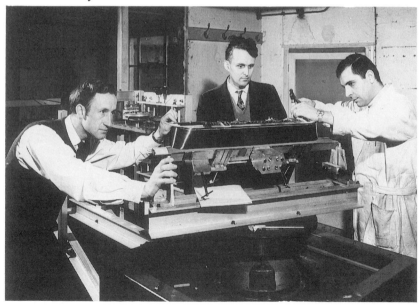

Anthony Costley-White (left) and Dr. Peter Hanley of Oxford Instruments make final adjustments to a hybrid magnet at Osney Mead in June 1973. Oxford Instruments, founded by Martin Wood in a garden shed in Northmoor Road, Oxford, in 1959, moved on to the Osney Mead estate in 1965. A new building was added in 1971 to rehouse electronic and cryogenic production facilities from Frank Cooper's old premises. (OCN)

The 'topping out' ceremony at the new Oxford Mail and Times building in Osney Mead in March 1970. Alderman Percy Bromley, the Lord Mayor of Oxford, passes a pint to Michael Doyle, one of the carpenters who had worked on the building. As a linotype operator at Newspaper House, Ald. Bromley had a more than passing interest in the project. (OCN)

Anthony Wood, alias Don Chapman, finds an appropriate way of moving from central Oxford to the new building at Osney Mead in February 1972. The fast-flowing river actually made the journey impossible and the boatman, Paul Hubbucks, only took the punt out a few yards for the photographer's benefit before returning to the landing stage at Folly Bridge. (OCN)

A stone column, one of 27 made for the prestigious new Covent Garden development in London, is hauled upright at Axtell, Perry and Symm's yard in Osney Mead in 1997. The premises in the background were built for the old-established firm Symm & Co. in 1969; Axtell and Perry's merged with Symm's in 1972 to create a firm with 25 stonemasons, probably more than any other firm in the Southern Counties. (MA)

Recreation

The small homes and gardens of West Oxford offered limited scope for recreation and it was always tempting to go outside. Ethel Fowler remembers Bridge Street in the 1920s when, 'All up the street in the summer, nearly all the women used to bring their chairs and sit in the front and chatter or do a bit of sewing or knitting.' In the 1940s, when Double Summer Time was in force, June Warne recalls people chatting outside their front gates in Alexandra Road until 10 p.m. Children could have friends round but few parents perhaps would have tolerated the lively games of hide and seek when June's friends sometimes became trapped in fallen wardrobes.

'I had five brothers and three of them got pinched for playing football in the Botley Road — fined five shillings each.' Norman Bunning's memories recall a time when most West Oxford children played in and around the street. There were seasonal games such as skipping, whips and tops, hoops, hopscotch or conkers. Ball games were rather more contentious and Gwen Ilsley and her friends, playing rounders at the corner of West Street and Swan Street, exasperated the usually good-natured Mrs Oakey by breaking two windows in one day. In Earl Street, Mrs Rowland would put an end to full-scale football matches by grabbing the ball and cutting it up with a big carving knife! Ann Allan remembers spending 'most of our time . . . playing games that consisted of getting across the road by various means' or doing handstands against the walls of houses. June Warne enjoyed playing marbles in the gutter or throwing cigarette cards. More annoyingly, New Botley lads gathered in the evenings to play hide and seek on the corner of Botley Road and Duke Street. Bill Stevens remembers that the shopkeeper, 'Poor old Ted Coulling, he used to complain to the police 'cos we was making that much row he couldn't hear what his customers was asking.' P.C. Page would hug the railings as he came along to sort them out but his white gloves generally gave him away and the boys would scarper quickly away down Duke Street or Earl Street.

From the street children progressed naturally to local recreation grounds and further afield. West Oxford's first recreation ground was to the north of the school in Ferry Hinksey Road, but temporary housing occupied this site in the early 1920s. Botley Road recreation ground was opened soon afterwards with swings and a sandpit near the main road and Oatlands Road recreation ground followed by 1930; finally, St John's College gave King George's Field to the City Council as a playing field in 1935. These areas provided formal play equipment and plenty of space for football, cricket and other sports; West Oxford Bowls Club was established at Botley Road rec in 1924 and the City constructed tennis courts there by 1937. Children explored tree houses at the edges of the fields or, like Jim Tyler in the 1910s, swam in the Bulstake Stream near

Botley Road. Beyond Willow Walk, which was opened up as a public path in 1923, children and families spent summer days at the Ducks and Pool. Gill Sawyer recalls, 'that [it] used to be lovely along there, it used to be like a little beach, the grass, and then the youngsters used to swim in that and then over in the Pool was the older people where you could swim.' At the age of about ten, Gwen Ilsley and her friends would 'go off p'raps to Henwood with a few jam sandwiches and a bottle of lemonade; we might be gone all day.' Ken Barrett, arriving in Oxford as a wartime evacuee, enjoyed birds' nesting expeditions into the surrounding countryside and fished the local streams with a homemade fishing rod or 'harpoon'. John Power remembers 'endlessly fishing' and fished by gaslight in East Street for great black tench that were attracted by the hot water from the power station opposite.

'What's the temperature at Tum?' was a popular springtime topic of conversation in West Oxford. Children from the local schools going for swimming lessons were generally allowed to walk across the allotments to Tumbling Bay bathing place, but other users were ferried across the main river by punt from a point just above Four Streams; there was no access from Botley Road rec until 1955. The bathing place had been created for males only in 1853 and a thousand people a day were visiting it in 1876. Women and girls were allowed to use the pool on Fridays from 1882 and a screened-off bathing place for women was formed in 1913. In the 1920s, Miss Long, supervisor of the women's pool, rigorously enforced segregation of the sexes. Joan Bates remembers that 'Some children came in carrying a baby and she wanted to know whether it was a boy or a girl and either they didn't know or they didn't tell her so she lifted up the child's clothes to find if it was a boy or a girl, found it was a boy and told them to take it out, they were not going to have it in a girls' bathing place.' Segregation had ended by the 1950s when Tum had slides and springboards at both ends and diving boards in the former men's pool. More than 86,000 admissions were recorded between May and September 1947 and Tum continued to be a popular destination for many summer outings until the age of heated pools and exotic holidays. It was officially closed in 1990.

There were several eagerly awaited events in the West Oxford calendar. On May Day in the 1920s, Osney children collected daisies in Payne's Field, the modern Osney Mead, and carried a hoop through the streets, receiving sweets from Granny Morris at her shop in Bridge Street. Until the 1950s, residents in Abbey Road and Cripley Road held a May Day dance on wasteland beside the river. St Giles' Fair provided further excitement since many vehicles parked in Ferry Hinksey Road before racing in to seize the best positions in St Giles' after midnight on Sunday. When the fair was over, some rides and sideshows came down to Payne's Field to provide a cheaper West Oxford version; most local people were delighted, but David Walker's mother, living in West Street, objected to endless repetitions of the song 'Oh, Johnny! Oh, Johnny! How you can love!' In the weeks leading up to Guy Fawkes' Night, boys would gather materials for giant bonfires in streets or on bits of wasteland. John Power remembers that the bonfire on the corner of West Street and Swan Street used to blister the paintwork on nearby front doors! Local rivalries were acted out and Bob Allen recalls his gang setting fire to the Friars' bonfire in the Oxpens a few days before November 5th; 'then we dashed up on to the footbridge that goes over the railway, Mill Street, the bottom of

Mill Street, and we watched it go up and the old fire engine come and then we got a bit frit … so we went home.' The Friars' gang took just two nights to retaliate!

Pubs, clubs and allotments occupied much local leisure time. John Power recalls Osney Town as 'a sort of sea of drink' because there were four pubs, the Waterman's, the Hollybush, the Swan and the Telegraph, as well as three off-licences. The Waterman's had social and sporting clubs and members of the cricket club put on amateur theatricals at the annual dinners. Ken Brookings and Charles Henderson ran a weight-lifting club in the old St Frideswide's School and, in the late 1930s, the Baptist Sunday School in Bridge Street became a social club offering 'a 3d Opera on Saturday night and 'Tramp Suppers' with fish and chips in paper'. Mrs Corby recalled that Frank Pakenham, later Lord Longford, was a one-time club member. In 1939, local people founded the West Oxford Democrats Club in the large North Street house where Francis Shepherd, of the Oxford tailoring firm, Shepherd & Woodward had lived. Another big house in North Street, the Manor House, where Osney children 'used to ring the bell and run away', became a club in 1953 when the Reform Club moved to Osney island from the city centre. In response to local demand, the City Council provided a huge number of allotments in West Oxford after the Allotments Act of 1887 and many families have benefited from them over the years. John Power, President of the local allotment association, was first taken over to the Twenty Pound Meadow allotments as a baby. Mary Walton remembers families from New Botley going to the old Bulstake allotments: 'In the evenings, spring and summer, you'd see the families come down on to the allotments and work together, the mother and the father and the children and everybody would be having a laugh and a joke with everybody and then they'd pick a bottle of beer up and all their cheese and biscuits and back home for supper… Small things were enjoyable in those days.'

The meadows of West Oxford attracted circus visits from Victorian times and Butlin's set up a funfair on the Botley Road recreation ground during the War as part of the City's 'Holidays at Home' scheme. The Oxford Ice Rink, built in Botley Road in 1930, was a much more ambitious facility and attracted huge crowds to ice dance shows and Varsity ice hockey matches. On such occasions, the area had a glimpse of a more congested future with cars parked in every side street and special buses serving all parts of Oxford. Many local residents took advantage of open evenings on Tuesdays and Thursdays when admission cost 1s 6d. The Ice Rink complex included a ballroom and the young Mary Walton at No. 115 Botley Road was able to serve in the shop wearing a white coat over her dress before nipping across the road for a night's dancing. Ice-skating could not compete commercially with the new 'talkies', however, and the Ice Rink was converted into a temporary cinema in 1933 before opening as the Majestic Cinema on 2 April 1934. The Mayor of Oxford, Ald. Miss Tawney, declined an invitation to attend because Mae West's film 'I'm No Angel' was so controversial. The cinema comfortably seated 2,500 people and Mary Walton's evenings out with her future husband cost just one shilling, 4d each admission, 2d for her bar of Cadbury's chocolate and 2d for his packet of Woodbines! The Majestic flourished until September 1940 when it was hurriedly taken over to provide temporary accommodation for refugees from the London Blitz. Frank Cooper Ltd. occupied the building between 1950 and 1967 and it became an MFI store until it was pulled down in 1986.

Shortage of money left many local people with little choice but to make their own entertainment. In the early 1930s, Colonel ffennell from Wytham Abbey gave the lads of New Botley a glimpse of another more affluent world, stopping his Cadillac to pay for Bill Stevens' gang to go skating in the Ice Rink. As Norman Bunning recalls, he also offered occasional lifts; 'He used to come down in his car, he had a big boot in the back and about twelve of us, we would all pile in and he'd take us from this street [Earl Street] to Botley Bridge and we had to get out and walk home. We used to think that was marvellous.'

Home and family

Members of the Mapleston family in the garden of No. 32 South Street in about 1900. Robert Mapleston, an engine driver with the G W R, was living in Osney Town with his wife, Elizabeth, by 1871. (JDW)

Wartime group in the garden of 'Hill View' in West Street in about 1942. The relaxed people, from left to right, are −, Jacqueline Keeler, Ted Badger, June Evans, Eva Money, −, Dot Evans, −. West Court now occupies the site of 'Hill View'. (DW)

Peter Taylor in the garden of No. 61 Mill Street in about 1956. (AA)

Two years old Olivia Graham washes the family car, a Hillman Imp, in Hill View Road in August 1979.

Pubs and clubs

The Osney Arms in Botley Road in the 1900s when the Hill View Road street sign was still perched on top of a pole. A few customers are evident, including an old man on the bench outside, and a notice beneath the bay window encourages passing cyclists to stop for a drink.

Members of the Waterman's social club gather round the landlord, T Hambridge (seated centre) in about 1932. Mr Hambridge is flanked by his father (left) and Mr Boyles (right) and his son, Cecil, is sitting on the pavement (left). Among those standing in the row behind the landlord are Mr Peart (left), Mr Barson (fifth from left) and Mr Coles (sixth from left); two women are visible in the background but they were not allowed to go on the club's outing. (RH)

Smiling faces in the bar of the Waterman's Arms pub in the 1950s. (RH)

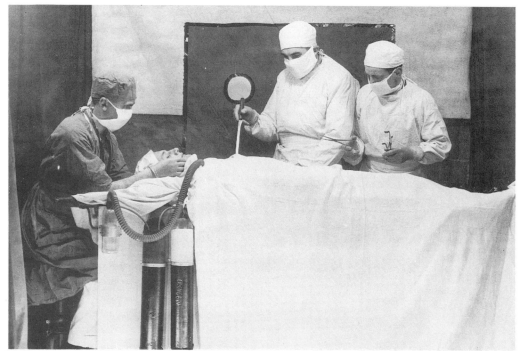

Osney Cricketers from the Waterman's provide dramatic entertainment during the club's annual dinner and social on 14 November 1953. This piece, entitled 'Operation Futile', starred, from left to right, David Walker (Anaesthetist), Archie Lawfull (The Patient), Bert Webb (1st Surgeon) and Jerry Brookings (2nd Surgeon). (RH)

Local people enjoy a faggot and peas supper in the yard of the Waterman's in the early 1950s. (RH)

Tom Parker, skipper of the 'Primrose', casts off as the Waterman's Arms Aunt Sally team sets off for a match against the Isis Hotel at Iffley in September 1975. The team lost 2–1 despite this unusual mode of transport and Tom Parker fell in the river twice on the way home. (OCN)

The Old Gatehouse Aunt Sally team celebrates winning Section 1 in September 1962. The happy faces belong to: front row, Bill Woodington (landlord), R F Tomkins, R Goodall, C Trafford (captain), M Greenaway, Mrs Woodington; back row, W Hayes, M Baker, W Bates, J Bowling and F Heritage. (OCN)

Mrs V Cooper of the Kite pub women's darts team gets in some practice for the coming season in August 1964. The three interested observers, from left to right, are Mrs J Longford, Mrs C Howkins and Mrs Y Lewis who played for the Plumber's Arms in St Ebbe's. (OCN)

Spectators enjoy themselves during an Aunt Sally game at the Democrats' Club in about 1958. The men standing at the back are, from left to right, Brian Slade, Reg Haffenden, Alf Slade, Harry Platt, Mr Sessions, Bob Webb; seated, from left to right, are Joan Clark, Mrs Clark, Dolly Slade, Renie Haffenden, Myrtle Slade, Mrs Sessions, Sam Wilchire, Cyril Morgan. (RH)

Alf Slade prepares to throw another wood during a game of Aunt Sally behind the Democrats' Club in North Street, Osney, in about 1958. The nissen hut in the background was built for dances and other functions after the War. (RH)

Members of the Reform Club bar billiards team at the clubhouse in Osney Town, in November 1977. The team had won the Oxford and District Bar Billiards Association Group A winter and summer knockout titles. Pictured with their trophies are, from left to right, Hughie Roberts, Roger Godfrey, Graham Micklewright, Roy Howard, Jack Rosie and Ivan Roberts. (OCN)

Oxford Ice Rink from Botley Road in the early 1930s. Designed by the local architect, J R Wilkins, and built by Kingerlee's, the building was opened on 7 November 1930 by the Mayor of Oxford, Captain G T Button, who skated across the ice to cut the ribbon. The rink was hugely popular but the talkies promised better financial

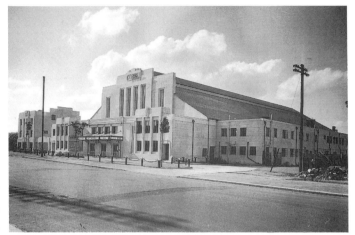

returns and the building was converted to become the Majestic cinema, 'the largest picture theatre in the South Midlands', in April 1934.

Allotments and parks

The Lord Mayor, Bill Fagg, and his wife are shown the Twenty Pound Meadow allotments after inspecting the new amenities shed in September 1975. The group includes, from left to right, Mrs Dutton, Harry Hemmings, Alf Dutton, Bert Standingford, Bill England, John Power, Ida Fagg, Derek Barnes, John Thomas, Bill Fagg, Charlie ('Wag') Brookings, secretary of the local allotments association, and Carmichael Wallace. (OCN)

Mark Goatcher takes a break from cultivating his allotment at the Oxford and Swindon Co-operative Society's depot in Ferry Hinksey Road in August 1975. He lived at the nearby lodge and was handily placed to grow most vegetables, including 'more rhubarb than I can handle.' King's Meadow now occupies this site. (OCN)

Members of the West Oxford Bowls Club on Botley Road Recreation Ground in the 1960s. Identified players include, from left to right: back row, −, Harvey Curtis, −, Bill Parsons, −, Phil Nye, Keith Monger, −, −, −; middle row, −, −, −, −, Fred Bunce, −, Bill Collett, −, Les West, −, −, −, Les Hearne, Edgar Martin, Fred Honour, Gordon Hallett; front row, James Tyler, − Cooper, −, Phil Pratley, Len Harding, Jock Murray, −, Bob Allen (landlord of the Osney Arms), −, Jim Tyler. (JL)

West Oxford Democrats Club football team in about 1965. The players, from left to right, are: back row, Bob Holt, Chris Broadway, B Wiggins, A Van-Gucci, Brendan Carter, W Moffet, J Baker, J Holt, R Longford, K Longford; front row, M Oliver, T Sculley, A Holt with T Merrick, D Merrick, R Bridges. (BC)

'Look at the camera!' A mother urges her son to forget the swing for a second at Oatlands Road Recreation Ground in about 1930. When the City Council first acquired this field as a recreation ground the playground equipment was placed near the houses between Oatlands Road and Harley Road.

Mavis Amos easily wins the 100 yards race at the fete on Botley Road Recreation Ground in about 1953. The gallant losers are, from left to right, Heather King, Dorothy Phillips, June Hartwell and June Hucker. (JDW)

A long way from the beach; June Hartwell poses in a swimsuit in the wide open spaces of Oatlands Road rec in 1963. (JDW)

Local youngsters letting off steam on Botley Road Recreation Ground during the West Oxford Community Association summer playscheme in 1976. (JL)

The goalkeeper is sent the wrong way during a penalty kick competition on Oatlands Road rec in 1977. The event took place during the Oatlands Road Silver jubilee celebrations and made good use of two concrete posts from the fence that formerly separated the public park from West Oxford School playing field. (JL)

Water

Herbert Taylor takes a dive into Tumbling Bay bathing place, perhaps in the 1900s. Nude swimming by men was accepted for many years since Oxford's bathing places were initially an all male preserve and they remained segregated after females were allowed to use them. Before Abbey Road was built, an eagle-eyed woman complained that she could see naked men at Tumbling Bay from the refreshment room at the Great Western railway station! (AA)

Ann, Peter and Susan Taylor with their dad, Philip, in the shallow end at Tumbling Bay in about 1958. The bathing place was hugely popular at this time and access for West Oxford people became easier in 1955 when an entrance was opened from the Botley Road rec. (AA)

Enthusiastic youngsters fill the diving boards at Tumbling Bay during the hot summer of 1959. The Oxford loco shed is visible in the background behind the changing cubicles; on the right, water is gushing over the lasher from the former women's pool. (OCN)

Misses E M and E B Matthews fish beside Osney Bridge in September 1964. Between them they had 80 years experience of fishing in the pool beneath the weir. (OCN)

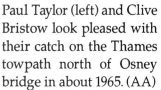

Paul Taylor (left) and Clive Bristow look pleased with their catch on the Thames towpath north of Osney bridge in about 1965. (AA)

Members of the West Oxford Angling Society show off their trophies in the Osney Arms pub in July 1977. The happy band includes, from left to right, Paul Taylor, Mick Alderson (club secretary), David White (match secretary), Geoff Nudd and Peter Mulford. (AA)

Enterprise dinghies from the Medley Sailing Club race on the Thames beside the Binsey poplars in about 1965. Founded in 1937, the club used the Port Meadow reach for competitive racing until Farmoor reservoir became available in 1966; more recently, it has become a family sailing club. (OCN)

Peter Graham takes a rubber dinghy out on the flooded Oatlands Road rec in February 1990.

Community life

A huge crowd attends the ox roast at Osney Lock which marked the Coronation of King Edward VII on 9 August 1902. The victim was a Hereford heifer which had been killed by Mr Bowell in Mill Street before being packed with large blocks of ice at the Oxford Ice Company's stores in Bridge Street. The carcase was taken to the site early on the 9th and carving of the meat began at 9.30 a.m.; by 1 p.m., everything was gone.

West Oxford scout troop gathers in Arthur Street in the shadow of the Osney Power station in the early 1920s. Bill Hartwell (born 1908) is standing just to the left of the two top drums. (JDW)

Coronation procession in Arthur Street in June 1953. Susan Taylor, pushing the pram, and her sister, Ann, to her right, were the Bisto kids in the local fancy dress competition; the girl in Welsh costume is Julia Snead. (AA)

Fancy dress competitors in front of the Botley Road Day Nursery during local celebrations of the Coronation of Queen Elizabeth II in June 1953. The children, from left to right, are Ann Davis, Paula Clarke, T Morris, — Morris, Brendan Carter and P Robins. (BC)

The cast of Red Riding Hood enjoys the applause after a performance at West Oxford Community Centre, the former St Frideswide's Boys' School, in February 1962. Edith Hartwell, standing on the right with a bouquet of flowers, organised and directed regular shows and pantomimes at the Community Centre from the late 1950s. (JDW)

June Hartwell's birthday party in West Oxford Community Centre in 1959. The group, with June seated in the middle, is posed in front of the wood and glass partition that had separated the school classrooms during lessons and folded back to create a large hall for assemblies and other events. Sixpenny hops were held here in the 1940s, featuring just a pianist and a drummer. (JDW)

The Oxford Caledonian Pipe Band leads a procession of floats along the Botley Road on 1 July 1967. Further on, the band nearly missed the entrance to Botley Road Recreation Ground and had to wheel sharply left, scattering the watching mothers and children as they did so. It made a memorable start to the West Oxford Community Association's first open air fete. (PS)

Miss West Oxford, Paula Hogg, and her attendants at West Oxford Community Centre on 1 July 1967. A 17 year old girl from No. 19 Bridge Street, Paula was crowned by the Lord Mayor, Alderman Frank Pickstock, before the Community Association fete. (PS)

Oatlands Road street party in June 1977 to celebrate the Silver Jubilee of Queen Elizabeth II. (JL)

Silver Jubilee street party in Cripley Place in 1977. Identified people include Noel Fitzsimmons, leaning against the wall, and, in the foreground (3rd, 4th and 5th from right), Sue Clarke, Jan Clarke and Ian Clarke. (BC)

Steve Nyman auctions off produce at the West Oxford summer fete in about 1978. The event was held on the Botley Road Recreation Ground. (JL)

Members of a tap dancing class at the West Oxford Community Centre in Binsey Lane in about 1985. The dancers are, from left to right: back row, Kate Allan, −, −, −, Helen Broadway, Katie Radbourne, Kelly Simms, −, Paulina Cartwright, −, −, Victoria Bartlett, Julie Young; middle row, Lucy Allan, Amy Driscoll, −, Maria Holmes, Helen Bagnall, −, Demelza Baker, −; front row, −, −, −, − (JL)